Section A

Introduction: Was it this week?

It's 12:45pm. Fifteen minutes to the end of French. Thirty minutes to the start of *Salt, but not Pepper,* the dynamic new name of the School's Christian group... which you're running. Yes, it had seemed weeks away when you'd agreed to run the meeting. Plenty of time to arrange your game/talk/video/guest speaker/performing acrobat. Well, it had been weeks away then. Now, however, it's fifteen minutes of pluperfect verbs followed by a swift demolition of a cheese and tomato roll and ten angst-ridden minutes of sweat and – God willing – inspiration.

It was perfectly OK for Peter not having to worry about what to say when put on trial. He was a disciple. A man of faith. He could rely on God giving him the right words at the right time. Perhaps God would do the same for you. On the other hand, as you wonder whether to use avoir or être, you can't help thinking that the whole point of preparation time was to allow you to prepare. Too late for that now, however, for the bell is about to ring. It's not often that you wish for lessons to last fifteen minutes longer...

Does the above scenario ring a bell (pardon the pun!) with you? Have you ever arrived at a meeting feeling completely under-prepared and needing to rely on a combination of Holy Spirit intervention and quick wits? If so, *Running Christian Groups in Secondary Schools* is for you. It looks at the purpose of such groups, considers their aims and promotes some good practice. It suggests ways in which you can be organised and prepared – yet still allow God's Spirit to work amongst the group. And it contains 40 different meeting outlines for a variety of types of group that are ready to use immediately, including:

★ *Christmas for all*
★ *Guidance for your Discipleship groups*
★ *Jesus – Who? for your Just Looking group.*

There are activities that will work with just a few pupils or with a few dozen. There are sessions to get your Christians thinking and sessions to introduce the whole concept of Christianity to those who have little or no church background. There are activities that require imagination and creativity as well as quieter spaces for prayer, reflection and Bible discussion.

Moreover, all the outlines are of a suitable length (45 minutes) for a lunchtime or short after-school meeting; nor is there the need to arrive with three food processors, a set of decanters and a life-size cuddly toy as is so often the way with church-based youth meeting outlines. Everything you will need is either enclosed in the book, easily accessible at school or able to fit into your school bag.

But even if you are not able to form or be part of a school group, do be encouraged that God is with you in your situation. He has called each one of us to serve him and to build relationships with those around us. We may not be the sort of people who like to be in up-front, highly visual positions. We may not feel that we have sorted out exactly what it means to be a Christian at school. The fact is, however, that God has called his people to be salt and light wherever they are and in whatever they are doing. As you build friendships with those whom God has placed around you, you are already responding to the opportunities that God has created for you to serve him in the school context.

Whatever you are looking for, we hope that you will find plenty to challenge and equip you in the following chapters and meeting outlines as you seek to serve God in school.

Simon Barker & Bruce Lockhart

Chapter one 1

Christian groups – why bother?

School is a busy place. Pupils desperately trying to get last night's homework completed. Teachers desperately trying to get last night's marking completed. The dash for the dinner queue. Changing for the sports clubs. Meetings. Lessons. Assemblies. More lessons. More meetings. It is as if you have climbed aboard a fearsome rollercoaster: you're on a journey full of violent ups and downs that are completely beyond your control, with no prospect of escape until you arrive dishevelled, disorientated and breathless, back where you started.

In this helter-skelter existence where, like Lewis Caroll's Queen of Hearts, it sometimes seems necessary to be going as fast as you can simply to stay in the same place, an obvious question for a Christian to raise is this: *How can I be a Christian at school?* Or, to put it another way, *How can I exercise my faith in a meaningful and relevant way at my school?*

Of course, for everyone who asks that question, there is a different answer. The Christian pupil might want to make a point about Creation in a science lesson; the Christian teacher might want to be sure that they are treating the pupils fairly; the Christian lunchtime supervisor might endeavour to serve the meals promptly while the Christian bursar will want to ensure that all financial matters are handled professionally. The school is a living community and within it God calls all Christians to serve him faithfully in their own particular ways.

Yet, within the school context, there are particular opportunities – and pressures – that make it useful for Christians to meet together on a regular basis. Of course, some Christians may feel that they get sufficient support outside the school, and some may not wish, or indeed be able, to attend a Christian group. But for the vast majority – and particularly for the pupils – a Christian group can be a very positive and significant event in their school lives. Consider:

★ *Sarah, a Year 8 pupil, is being picked on for being a Christian. The group is the one place she can go to receive support, encouragement and prayer.*

★ *Steve is in Year 11 and, along with his parents, attends a small village church where he is the only person aged over 10 and under 34. The Christian group is the place where he receives fellowship with people of his own age and the encouragement of knowing he is not alone.*

★ *Paul is in Year 7. He's always listened carefully to the Vicar at his Primary School assemblies and now he has just been given a Gideon's Bible. At a Christian group, he can ask about how to read it and what it might mean.*

★ *Sophie's grandfather has recently died. Although she has never been to church, she had been praying for him to get better and now blames God for his death. At a Christian group she can raise her questions and begin her search for answers.*

★ *Neil is doing A level RE. They have been studying the nature of suffering and Neil isn't quite sure how what he is learning can be reconciled with what his faith has taught him. At the group, he can work through those issues.*

★ *Brian and Liz went to an event in the school hall last month, organised by some of the local churches. Brian became a Christian there but Liz still has questions. With no church links, the group can be a vital place for their support and growth.*

★ *Peter is concerned that some of his form are getting into ouija boards and fortune-telling. He knows it's wrong but doesn't really know why. The group can help him find out more information as well as pray for those who are involved.*

★ *John is keen to share his faith with anyone who'll listen. He is frustrated that assemblies are devoid of any mention of God and that Christianity seems to have no impact on the daily life of the school. The group could be a place where events – or even assemblies – could be planned that do have a positive impact at school.*

Of course, no one group is going to meet the needs of all these people. In fact, if they all turned up on the same week, the chances are that several, if not most, would leave disappointed. And that is the first important point to grasp.

No Christian group can hope to be all things to all men – or all women. Obviously, there is no point in running a different club for each type of person; you wouldn't have the time or the manpower anyway and, more to the point, there is great benefit in people meeting together who come with different perspectives and questions. But do not feel that you need to be trying to run a group that will be everything for everyone. Just as a church has different events for toddlers and the elderly as well as prayer meetings and Christian outreach meetings, so a Christian group is likely to be selective in its purpose and target audience.

But as it is probable that a group will draw people who are either of a similar age or who come with a similar purpose, some schools do run more than one type of group so that they can meet the needs of a wider range of pupils. Often they will run just one group on a regular basis (though from time to time its purpose and therefore target audience will change) and then, as need or circumstance arise, they will run another one for a limited time.

So what are some of these different types of group? Let's look at a few possibilities:

Bible Reading Cell Group

This type of group has become increasingly popular over the past few years. Pupils meet together for the sole purpose of reading the Bible together – an activity which, if we're really honest, we all struggle with from time to time. They might follow set notes or simply start at Genesis (or Matthew) and keep going. A typical group would pray before it starts and then read a chapter at a time, either sharing out the reading or having one person read while the others follow/listen (depending on the number of Bibles and ability of readers). At the end of each chapter they would pause to reflect on it and to ask questions that the passage has raised.

The Discipleship Group

This group would consist predominantly – if not exclusively – of committed Christians and would tend to draw from the older ages. This group would be comfortable spending time in worship, Bible study (of meaty topics!) and prayer, and might look for ways that it could put God on the agenda of the whole school.

The Just Looking Group

This group would target those who want to explore the Christian faith but who have no personal faith yet. They would address such issues as Who is God?, What is sin?, etc as well as answering questions that the group members themselves might bring. The programme would be fairly interactive with more of an emphasis on learning by doing than by reading.

Mix and Match

To some extent most groups have a combination of different types of people, but this group would have a balance of Christians and non-Christians, and of older and younger pupils. In many ways, although these groups are perhaps the most widespread, they are also the most difficult to run effectively. It is not easy to settle on a programme that will stretch the more mature without going over the heads of the younger ones, while a programme that gets no further than the basics will not stretch those who need stretching.

For the purpose of this book, we have divided the outlines in Section B into three types of groups:

★ *Just Looking*
★ *Mix and Match*
★ *Discipleship Group*

The *Just Looking* meeting outlines focus on the basics of the Christian faith with more of an emphasis on activity than writing or discussion – yet the outlines do get to grips with the Bible and what God has done through Jesus.

The *Mix and Match* outlines are issue-based and focus on those areas that teenagers wrestle with (peer pressure, parents, relationships, etc) and approaches them from a Christian perspective. They have a balance of activities alongside Bible-based questions and discussion starters.

The *Discipleship Group* outlines cover some deeper issues that will stretch those who have been Christians for some time. The emphasis here is more on prayer, Bible study and discussion with searching questions that may challenge both belief and behaviour.

On top of these three, we have also included ten specials: outlines on some of the key events of the year, including Christmas, St Valentine's Day, Easter and Hallowe'en. Most Christian groups want to cover these topics at some stage and so these allow you to do so. Their format is closer to that of the *Mix and Match* group.

Of course, you do not need to feel restricted by our suggestions. With a bit of planning and creative adaptation, you could make a *Just Looking* outline suitable for your older or more spiritually mature group, or vice versa. The important thing is that you look through the material carefully beforehand and ensure that it is appropriate for *your* group. If this means missing bits out, adding bits in or reorganising the bits into an order that suits you better, that's fine. Please don't let the meeting outlines restrict you and your own creativity. Rather let them be springboards that start you off on a path that will bring the reality of God to your group.

Chapter two ②

10 steps to getting started

Quite how you go about getting a group started will depend on who you are. For example, if you are a Head of Year or even the Head, matters such as getting permission to start up should not prove too difficult. On the other hand, if you are a pupil, even contemplating trying to see the Head of Year may fill you with dread and fear. And if you are a minister or youth worker, you may even be wondering what a Head of Year is or does.

So, a word of explanation: in this chapter, not everything will apply in quite the same way to everyone. Some bits will be relevant to your situation, others can be passed over. So engage brain, put on those glasses of discernment and work your way through the 10 steps to getting started, taking notes as you go. There will be a test at the end!

1. Getting praying

'The prayer of a righteous man is powerful and effective', asserts James (James 5:16). That of a righteous woman, equally so. Therefore, if you are thinking of getting a Christian group up and running, your starting point must be prayer. Time and again the Bible speaks of the importance of prayer and this is particularly important when you are considering a new Christian work in what is likely to be quite a difficult environment. You need to pray for wisdom, for God to oversee all the practical hurdles that face you, and to pray that this really is what God wants you to do. There's no point trying to do something because it seems like a good idea to you when it doesn't seem like a good idea to God. Check out Psalm 127, verse 1.

2. Getting together

Once you have felt a call to get things going, the next stage is to meet up with others. This could be with some of the older Christian pupils, with Christian teachers, with local ministers or youth workers or, ideally, with a combination of all of these. Spend time in prayer but also decide who is going to take responsibility for organising the planning and the meetings. Perhaps there is a teacher who is keen to be involved or perhaps there are older pupils who can manage with guidance and overseeing from teachers/youth workers.

This initial meeting could take place during school time but it would be better to meet at a home one evening; there is less pressure on time and the more relaxed atmosphere will allow you to chat, pray and think more openly.

3. Getting a vision

Probably your most important decision is to think about which pupils you particularly want the group to reach. It is extremely difficult to have one group that will be effective for everyone from Years 7 – 13 and which will provide support for Christians as well as be an outreach to non-Christians. What will be your main aim? Evangelism? Mutual support? Teaching? Who do you really hope will come? As you read through Chapter 1, you may already have felt a particular pull in one direction. Now is the time to ensure that everyone who will be involved is of the same mind.

Of course, a programme exclusively for a sixth-form group will look very different to the programme for a mainly Year 7 and 8 group but, wherever you feel God is calling you, there are a number of steps, common to all, which need to be followed as you start, regardless of the age/Christian background of those you hope will attend.

4. Getting permission

Following your initial meeting, you will need to approach the school to ask permission for the club to run on school premises and, possibly, during school time. You will almost certainly need to have a teacher who will agree to take responsibility for the group. Ideally, this would be a Christian teacher who can provide very active support and guidance, but you may have to manage with a sympathetic teacher who is happy just to put their name to the club.

Schools vary about who you need to ask permission from. In some, you will need to approach the Head or Principal, whereas in others it may be a Deputy Head or even a Head of Year. In any case, before you meet with the relevant person it is important that you have thought through the issues outlined in this chapter. You are far more likely to get approval if you can show that you have thought carefully about some of the details of the group, rather than coming with vague 'pie in the sky' ideas.

Remember that schools are places of education and, although your club is a voluntary one, Heads can get nervous if they think that what is going on in a club is too way out.

You also need to remember that if the Head closes the club for any reason, it may be many years before it will be able to restart and much damage can be done to the Christian presence in the school in the meantime.

On the other hand, many Heads are extremely positive about a Christian group in the school. This may just be because it looks good in the school prospectus, but it may equally be that Heads are very keen to promote spiritual values in their school and they can see the positive influence that a healthy Christian group may have.

5. Getting a room

One of your most obvious needs is the one for a suitable venue. Where will you meet? Is there a Christian teacher who will let you use their form room? Or will the form want to be in there if it is a wet lunchtime? It is not ideal to be in a room where you are going to be constantly disturbed or interrupted but, on the other hand, there is no advantage to being tucked away in the remotest corner of the school where even Indiana Jones, complete with a detailed map, would struggle to find you.

If you are hoping for a cross-section of ages to come, then where you meet can be very significant. Some younger pupils might find entering a sixth form block something akin to a wildebeest turning up at a lions only convention, while some middle school pupils might be equally reluctant to go back to the lower school block. Is there a place that might offer comfortable chairs? Will you be able to get access to a video if you need one? Some groups like to be based near the RE area so that they can have access to Bibles.

Of course, it is highly unlikely that any one room will prove ideal for all these criteria, but it is worth thinking this issue through carefully before coming to a decision.

6. Getting a time

This may not be quite so obvious as it sounds. The majority of groups tend to meet at lunchtimes but there is a sizeable minority that meet after school and, believe it or not, even one or two that meet *before* school! Meeting at lunchtimes has the advantage of being sure that all the pupils are at least in school, but this doesn't necessarily mean that they are all available.

★ *There may be so many other clubs running that you are squeezed out by the competition.*
★ *It may be that your lunchtimes are so short that it is not worth meeting then.*
★ *It may be that your lunch arrangements are such that people are constantly having to come and go.*

Meeting after school means that you are not restricted by time quite so much and it may also mean that you can use a room that may not have been available at lunchtime. Of course, if the school has not given you permission for a Christian group on its premises, there is nothing to stop you meeting after school at someone's home. You do need, however, to think of transport – how are people to get home if they miss the school bus?

7. Getting a name

Once you have fixed up when and where you are going to meet, the next stage is to come up with a name for your group. This may seem to be quite a small point but it is worth thinking about the message that a name suggests. The *Come and Learn about Jesus* club may reflect what you hope might happen but, as a name, I can't see hordes of teenagers stampeding down the corridors just to get there. One group wanted to be *The Bible Bashers* – using the title ironically – but again it is important to think through what message this might convey to parents or visitors to the school. Some recent examples of group names that have worked well are:

The Rock	*Footsteps*	*Crossroads*
X-plore!	*Discovery*	*Solid*
Sorted	*The Forum*	*JAM (Jesus and Me).*

Others have picked up on the *WWJD* (What Would Jesus Do?) idea or taken their name from current films, TV shows or music. Whatever you finally settle on, make sure that it is one that is not going to cause offence or misunderstanding.

8. Getting known

These days it is quite easy to produce some fairly professional looking A4 posters simply by using a desk-top publishing package and a colour printer. These can be useful for letting everyone in school know about what is going on. Again, however, make sure that you ask permission to put up posters if that is required. If you are able, it is also worthwhile putting notices in registers and even arranging to give it a plug at assembly times as the day of your first meeting approaches.

Actually, however, most people will come through personal invitation and so it is well worthwhile spending some time brainstorming a list of names of those you know who may be interested. This is when contact with local churches can be useful as they can let you know the names of those pupils who attend church/youth groups. It would be good to send posters to the local churches so that they can be advertised at these youth groups and so that the churches can also be praying for you. (Churches can also prove to be useful contacts for resources and/or guest speakers once you get started.) Once you have a list of names, it would be good to write them a personal invitation but also to follow this up with a face-to-face conversation.

9. Getting a programme

The following chapter deals in much more detail with this but at this stage it is worth mentioning that you do need to have one! Of course, your programme doesn't want to be so tightly planned that you can't deal with suggestions/issues that arise from your first meeting, but there is no point trying to come up each week with a new idea on a Monday for your meeting on Tuesday.

Some groups like to plan a theme that runs for a half-term; others might intersperse their themes with special events – videos, guest speakers, etc. Others might follow particular books or courses, but whatever it is that you decide to do, it is important that you have a clear sense of what you want to achieve in the first few weeks, even if the vision – and programme – need to be refined in the light of what actually happens.

10. Getting underway

When the day comes for your first meeting, it would be good for a group of you to get together either before school or even at break to pray and just to confirm that you are organised. You then want to make sure that you arrive at the meeting room first so that you can get it arranged the way you want.

★ *Putting chairs into a circle can be a lot more welcoming than straight lines.*
★ *If you are providing drinks and biscuits then you need to organise this.*
★ *What about Bibles?*
★ *Do you need the video or an OHP or the white/blackboard?*
★ *Have you got pens and paper?*

The main priority of your first session must be to welcome everyone who comes and make them feel at home. Relationship is far more important than programme. Please don't feel that you need to give a lengthy exposition on the value of the cleansing laws in Leviticus. Instead, try to learn everyone's name and try to discover why they have come and what they hope to get from the group. This information can certainly help you as you plan for future weeks. It would be good, too, to share a little of your own hopes and expectations and perhaps close with a time of prayer, if appropriate.

Finally, make sure that you finish in time for everyone to get to their lesson/registration on time and for you to get the room back to how it was when you first arrived – or cleaner! It is well worth getting a good reputation for this so that you will be allowed to continue to use the room and so that when the odd minor blip occurs, it will be seen as just that.

Summary

The following diagram may well be a helpful way of summarising the preparations that are needed to get your Christian group up and running. There are three main ingredients: prayer, planning and publicity. Without spending time on all three of these areas, you are likely to struggle. Of course, the three are interdependent – you need to pray over your publicity and planning and your publicity will need to be discussed at your planning meetings. But it is vital that none of these areas are overlooked and that people take on responsibility for each of them.

PRAYER

PLANNING

PUBLICITY

Chapter three ③
Getting the right programme

Getting a Christian group started is both challenging and fun. The opportunity to explore the truths of the gospel with young people is not one to be missed. But in order for the group to work successfully, it is important to run with a programme that is suitable for those who come. There wouldn't be much point in running a course for adults on how to use a knife and fork without getting food everywhere (or perhaps there would!) because most adults have been doing that with a reasonable degree of success for many years. Nor would you expect a collection of pre-school children to sit patiently through a university-style lecture. The point is simply that you need to make sure that both the *content* of the sessions and the method of *presentation* are appropriate for those who come.

Having thought about the type of group that you are running (see Chapter 1), you need to start by focusing on two particular questions:

★ *What do I know about those who come?*
★ *What is the purpose (aim) of the group?*

Younger pupils tend to prefer a more active time and often learn by doing, whereas older pupils tend to prefer discussion-based activities. They are also able to cope with more abstract thinking while younger pupils need more concrete examples to help them understand ideas. If there are those with special needs or a group of poor readers, then the programme needs to ensure that they are not excluded and that there is sufficient time for everyone to complete the activities. It is far better to have a simple programme that can be achieved within the time-frame than to rush through a host of activities that are left unfinished or unexplained.

If your purpose is mutual support, then more time will be spent chatting and praying, whereas if your purpose is evangelistic, then more time will be spent in looking at the Bible and the claims of Christianity. For example, a more mature group may read the story of the lost son (Luke 15) and consider how they can become more like the father or how they would respond to the older son. For a younger group, where your aim is more evangelistic, you might want

them to act out the story and then focus on the father's love and the younger son's desire for forgiveness.

Once you have thought about those who will come and have decided on your purpose, it is a good idea to come up with a *theme* that you can follow for either a half-term or a whole term. Some examples include Addictions (drugs, alcohol, smoking, etc), Fruits of the Spirit (love, joy, etc), World Issues (the environment, fair trade, etc). Of course, within the theme, you can have one-off specials (such as Harvest or St Valentine's Day), but it is good to give the meetings a feel of continuity.

Even within the theme, however, each weekly topic can be approached slightly differently so that the programme continues to feel fresh.

Although people do like a sense of structure and the feeling of security this brings, *variety* is important. You can change the set-up of the room, the timings, and the order of events or introduce new ideas such as a video, drama or a guest speaker. Other suggestions for bringing new life to your old group are given in the following chapter.

Here are some programmes of different groups – with different ages and purposes – that may help you decide what will be the right format for your group. The timings below are approximate and may vary from outline to outline:

Just Looking
(A younger group; aim: evangelistic)
Tuning in
Welcome and opening activity linked to the theme – 10 min
Play
Main activity (centred on the theme) – 15 min
Pause
The Bible bit – 10 min
Fast forward
Response (Activity) – 10 min

Mix and Match
(A mix of ages; aim, teaching on life issues)
Tuning in
Welcome and opening activity linked to the theme – 10 min

Pause
Bible input and activity – 15 mins
Play
Follow-up activity – 15 mins
Fast forward
Response (activity/prayer) – 5 mins

Discipleship group

(An older group: aim, teaching/worship)
Tuning In
Prayer, worship – 10 mins
Play
Activity – 10 mins
Pause
Bible study/discussion – 20 mins
Fast forward
Response (worship, prayer) – 5 mins

Of course, these three outlines are just suggestions: you need to tailor these to your particular situation. You may have less (or more) time available. The restrictions on your room may mean that some activities are more difficult to manage. Some groups like to start with drinks and chat and use this as their *Tuning in* time. What is important is that you think carefully about who is coming to your group and about what your aim for the meeting is, and then organise your programme around this.

Remember, though, that the programme is there only to help you achieve your aim. If you are not doing that, then you need to adapt your programme and not simply follow it like a blinkered horse in a horserace. Take time to pause and evaluate every few weeks in order to consider what areas you need to alter/expand/drop/ introduce, etc. Even if you feel that things are going well, it will still be necessary to make occasional changes to avoid becoming stale and getting into a rut.

Chapter four 4
Spicing up your programme

Are you a fan of Chinese or Indian food? It's really good to go out for a meal or a take away and to eat something a bit different now and again. But, of course, if you did this every night, the food and the novelty would soon wear off and you'd get bored with eating the same thing time and time again. If you're not careful, going to the Christian meeting could easily become just like this.

When you start, everything is new and exciting – it's different and there's an energy around that comes from the buzz of the young people getting to grips with a dynamic, challenging programme. But before too long, energy levels start to drop and comments such as 'boring' creep in. People gradually vote with their feet and numbers start to drop.

The young people come with enthusiasm and a desire and need to be stimulated. The programme therefore needs to inspire them to interact with its content. When things go wrong, it isn't because the young people have lost their energy and enthusiasm, it is because the programme is no longer inspiring them to display these qualities. The question is, how do you avoid this happening, or, if you are faced with this situation already, what can you do to turn it around?

Keep them in suspenders!

Young people get bored when they know exactly what is going to happen next. So, one good tactic is to keep them in suspense. From time to time you can drop in a new or surprise item that will keep them on their toes. This doesn't mean that you throw out your structure or routine but it does mean that it needs to be flexible enough to cope with some (un)scheduled spontaneity.

At its most simple level, this spontaneity may be in changing the order of your programme or even the layout of your room (in the summer you could even go outside!), but there are other possibilities:

Drama: If you normally read your Bible bit, why not act it out or use *The Dramatised Bible?* Moreover there are loads of drama books with sketches that can be put on with minimal sets/props and with little rehearsal. Check out your local Christian bookshop for ideas. Or why not improvise? Young

people are extremely good at acting out impromptu short scenarios or role-plays – so give them the opportunity!

Poetry/quotes: Are there poems that will help to introduce or illustrate a point? Or are there comments or quotations that you can use to suggest alternative views? These can really help to stimulate discussion amongst an older group.

Speakers: Is there someone in the local area who would be able to come in and speak at your meeting? This may be a local youth worker who is a good communicator or it may be someone who has specialist knowledge of a topic. If you are looking at abortion or euthanasia, is there a Christian doctor who could help? Do make sure, however, that you get permission beforehand for guests to come and that they sign in on arrival.

Music: The words to many current songs can be an ideal lead-in to a discussion. The statements about life, love and God can be used effectively to stimulate thought. You may be able to borrow a tape/CD player from the school. There is also a lot of good Christian music too and you can be playing some of this while people arrive or when other activities are going on.

Worship: If you have a musician in your midst, you may want to sing some worship songs, but do make sure that you also have the words available. These could be incorporated into an opening time of praise or perhaps as a personal response to the teaching. Even if you don't have a musician, you could try singing unaccompanied or joining in with a track played on tape/CD.

Video: There are lots of Christian videos that can bring Bible stories to life – you could try hiring from a local Christian bookshop or borrowing from local churches. Alternatively, you can use clips from films or TV programmes to introduce or tie in with your theme for the day. Make sure that you have already got a TV and video booked and that your clip is lined up beforehand.

Challenges: Rather than throwing out your whole programme and starting again from scratch, you can breathe new life into what you do already by introducing some games or short challenges. These can be set, either for a bit of fun or as a way of illustrating a point that you want to make as a part of the programme. In fact, one group brought in a *Fun Spot* and then built on the idea for their whole programme, introducing such as items as the *Hot Spot* (interviews) and the *Think Spot* (Bible bit). Another group took the idea of boxes and had the *Joke Box, Brain Box* and *Soap Box,* amongst others.

Outings: One of the best ways for your group to gel together is by going somewhere – or doing something – together. This could mean all going round to someone's house one evening for a pizza or a video or it could involve going out on a trip such as ice-skating or ten-pin bowling. You will soon notice the difference in the quality of the relationships between group members once you have done something like this.

Just as important as any of the above, however, is the need to give your group members a voice and a feeling of ownership. They need to feel that they are encouraged to make suggestions and that their ideas are listened to and taken seriously. It is good too if they can be encouraged to take on responsibilities for various jobs – organising publicity, booking the TV, getting the Bibles, providing the biscuits, etc. A group that gets on well together and feels that it is responsible for the programme it runs is a group that stays together and grows together.

Chapter five 5
Managing your group effectively

'Order and our group just do not go together', commented one leader recently after seeing her session disintegrate into a series of small group conversations on topics as diverse as the previous night's *Eastenders*, the chances of United winning the title and the latest Leonardo Di Caprio film. Why had her planned discussion on the Trinity gone so far off track? Why did it seem so difficult to get people to concentrate? Was it all her fault? Or theirs? What could be done about it?

Creating the right atmosphere

The two biggest restraints on running a school group are undoubtedly time and place. Lunchtime groups rarely have more than 45 minutes and many have an awful lot less. How do you make the most of this time? Most groups take place in classrooms where chairs and desks are often laid out in rows and where notices advocating good behaviour (with the threat of dire punishments) adorn the walls. In the ideal world, it's probably not the time or place you would choose.

Still, all is not lost and it is possible to create a helpful atmosphere with just a few minutes preparation. Putting chairs into a circle is much more welcoming than having rows and a colourful poster for the club on the black/whiteboard can provide a helpful focus. If you are able to organise squash and biscuits and even allow people to eat their sandwiches as they arrive, you are a long way towards getting off on the right foot. It is well worth arriving five minutes earlier in order to get the room looking right for when people start arriving.

It is also important to have a formal start time so that those who come late aren't disturbing you by wanting to eat and drink once the activities have got underway. If you don't stick to this, people tend to arrive later and later so that you spend more time on your physical than spiritual food!

Group dynamics

God has created each one of us differently. Depending on whom you have in mind, that might be seen as a bad thing, but at least you can be grateful that we're not all like Kevin Armstrong. Bless him! Whereas on a TV/video player you have some control over *pause, stop* and *volume control*, Kevin is permanently locked on to *fast forward* at top volume. And you have three of him in your group! What can you do?

When Jesus chose his disciples, they seemed to be a very mixed and motley crew. Different homes, different families, different jobs, different personalities. They did not make the best students. At times they failed to understand simple truths and on one occasion they even argued about who was the most important. And yet Jesus loved them, cared for them, nurtured them and then left the entire fate of the Christian church in their hands. While the responsibility for the future of Christianity certainly does not lie exclusively in your hands, it would be good, however, to try to develop the nurturing and caring aspect of Jesus' ministry with your own group.

You could argue, of course, that Jesus actually had it easy. After all, at least he did get to choose his disciples whereas you have absolutely no control over who does, or doesn't, come to your group. How do you go about encouraging, motivating and, at times, disciplining those who attend? How would Jesus have dealt with Kevin?

Undoubtedly, the key starting point is *prayer*. You need to pray that you will have the same love and compassion for those who come, as God has. In the case of some individuals, this may not come easily – you might well be praying that they don't come at all! – but over time God will give you a heartfelt concern for those in your care.

Alongside the prayer, however, you need to have some strategies that will help the group to function smoothly and enable you to achieve the purposes that you intend.

★ *Clear guidelines: At the outset, make it perfectly clear what is and isn't acceptable while the group is running. These will vary from group to group depending on each situation, but people actually feel safer and more relaxed when they know where the boundaries lie. If the group is small, you may not need too many guidelines to start with but, as numbers increase, it will become more important to have some clear ground rules.*

★ *Encourage and encourage: Make every effort to*

encourage people to contribute constructively. If you praise good behaviour and helpful contributions you are far less likely to get the distractions you don't need. Try to be as positive as you can in your comments and in the way that you treat people; a smile, a pause or a raised eyebrow are more encouraging ways of ensuring that attention is restored than a critical comment or a raised voice.

★ ***Stick to the rules:*** *If you let people get away with breaking your rules, they will continue to do so and will push the limits even further. So, for example, if no one is allowed into the room before you arrive, send out anyone who has already gone in. If people start being silly once the session has started, then you can assume that they've also just volunteered to put the room straight at the end.*

★ ***Use sanctions:*** *With minor incidents, it is easy just to make those responsible tidy the room or do some small task, but what about those who constantly cause trouble or do something more serious? Firstly, be assured that it is quite in order to ask someone to leave. As a voluntary club, they do not have to be there and you do not need to have them. You can exclude them for a week (or longer) if you so choose. While this may seem to be a negative step, you cannot allow one or two individuals to spoil the meeting for the whole group.*

Also, remember that this is a *school* group. So any serious incidents should be reported to a Head of Year (or equivalent) and any matters of discipline will then become their responsibility. Never feel that you are fighting a lone battle – schools are very experienced in dealing with individuals who are disruptive and you will find them very sympathetic and helpful to your situation.

The different personalities

Often, however, managing the group is not a matter of discipline, it is more of a matter of dealing with the Kevins of this world at the same time as a range of other equally loveable and distinctly unique individuals...

The Know-It-All

Exodus? Can recite it backwards. Spring Harvest? Got the mug and the T-shirt. There seems to be no topic or idea that they haven't done already and they delight in telling you so. What can you do to stop them dominating the whole meeting?

★ *Don't put them down in front of the group but thank them for their input.*

★ *Ask questions to specific individuals so that others can contribute.*

★ *Gently interrupt and ask others for their opinions.*

★ *Give them a job that takes them out of circulation for a few minutes.*

The Bashful One

Who is she? Why is she here? Lucy has been coming for four weeks now and hasn't yet said a word. Whenever you look at her, her eyes shoot down to the floor. Help!

★ *Respect the fact that some personalities are naturally quiet and shy.*

★ *Ensure that there are elements of the programme where she can contribute.*

★ *Speak to her personally – thank her for coming, ask her to help you with a task.*

The Objector

Whatever it is, they don't want to do it. Not interested. Disaffected.

★ *Try to include an activity or a topic that does interest them.*

★ *Try to find out why they are being so disinterested.*

(I once discovered that a lad only came because his parents made him. He didn't want to be there and was looking to distract others. I suggested that he stopped coming and I spent time with him at other points of the week. A phone call to the parents helped them to understand my position.)

The Disagreer (Red Herring Merchant)

'But what about this or that?' 'How do you know?' 'No, it isn't!' 'Where's that bit about...?'

All these comments could be perfectly fair and come as a natural part of the discussion. On the other hand, there are those characters who will look for every opportunity to derail the topic of conversation on to their particular hobby-horse, or who may simply be trying to put you off by objecting to everything or asking irrelevant questions.

★ *Decide if it is a legitimate question or simply a ploy to distract you.*

★ *Thank them for their question and invite them to see you at the end for an answer.*

★ *Provide a Question Box and ask the group to put their comments in there.*

If you lead a group for long enough you will almost certainly see some of the above characters – and more besides – though you will be extremely unlucky if you happen to have them all at the same time. Leading a small (or large) group is a skill that takes years of practice and each group always throws up its own distinctives. There are, however, a good number of books around that can help you with this and it will be well worth your time reading a few as well as talking to some people who have had experience of leading such groups themselves.

What, there's more?

Chapter six **6**

aAfter a group has been meeting together for some time, it often comes to a point where it wants to have more of an impact on the life of the school. It is all too easy for the Christian group to become the Black Hole of school life. Of a lunchtime, a few individuals disappear into it each week only to emerge 40 minutes later with no visible sign of change. Where did they go? What did they do? What was the point?

As Christians, God has called us to be salt and light for him (Matthew 5:13–16). We cannot do that if all the Christians meet together simply to support, encourage and pray for one another, valuable as those things are. No, a truly effective Christian group is one that is able to support its members but one that also wants to impact the life of the whole school.

Of course, this is not necessarily an easy thing to do but it is important that the group does not become so turned in on itself that it fails to see the possibilities it has to put God and his good news on the agenda for the whole school. This can be done in a whole range of ways and the following are just suggestions of ways that have been successful in a number of schools over the past few years.

1. Personal stand

The starting point for any involvement beyond the group meeting must be with the day-to-day lives of the group members. They must be encouraged to share and to be God's good news in their school lives. In practice this may mean voicing a Christian viewpoint in lessons or questioning assumptions or ideas that go against their beliefs (books in the library?). It must also mean following Jesus' example and befriending and caring for those who are in need, perhaps by getting alongside an unpopular classmate or defending someone against bullying.

2. Church links

The Christian community in school does not exist in isolation. It is actually a part of a world wide Church and it is a good idea to build links with the local branches. Are there special events or services that local churches are putting on which you can invite friends to? Are there any joint youth celebrations in your area? It is important to have churches' prayer support for your group but these links can also be good opportunities for you to support their initiatives too.

3. School links

It is easy to think that your school group is the only one that is faced with the particular pressures and concerns that you have. Churches and youth workers can be supportive but at times you may feel that even they do not fully understand the distinctives of your situation. That is why it is good to meet together with Christian groups from other local schools. Often this can be a great way of receiving– and giving – encouragement as well as breaking down the feelings of mistrust or even antagonism that can exist between local/rival schools. Some areas have organised termly joint school celebrations and separate meetings for leaders to chat, plan and pray. (These meetings or events would probably take place outside of school as your school might not appreciate other pupils coming on to the premises during school hours.)

4. Hands on

Much of what goes on in school Christian groups can seem to have little visible effect in the long-term: 'It was a good assembly but it was last week...' 'The mission went really well but it was last term...' It is worth looking out for a project that will enable your group to do something that will have a lasting, positive effect. Is there a common room that needs redecorating or an area outside that could be reclaimed or put to good use for all the pupils? Perhaps there are practical things that you can do in the community.

5. Open meetings

Along with holding your regular meetings, it is good occasionally to put on a special event. Christmas and Easter obviously provide ideal opportunities but at any time you can hold debates on topical events or lay on a *Roast a Christian* (grill a panel about their beliefs on a range of issues) or hold an interview with a Christian teacher if one is prepared to be involved.

6. Taking assemblies

For many teachers, the prospect of taking an assembly is not one that sends them rushing to the Hall with enthusiasm. Therefore if your group offers to put on an assembly that is well prepared and is suitable in terms of its content and method of presentation, the suggestion is generally well received and taken up. *(Warning:* Anyone wanting to invite pupils forward if they wish to be washed in the blood of the lamb or to lay on an activity whereby the Head unexpectedly – but hilariously – gets covered in the lunchtime leftovers need not apply!) The Appendix offers a list of books which you could use for assembly ideas, and which also suggest how to go about putting them on.

7. Special events

Events such as Children In Need or Red Nose Day provide a great opportunity for the Christian group to get involved in a very positive way. Can you put on an event or activity that will support these causes? One school group took responsibility for delivering roses on Valentine's Day while another organised a Christmas card postal service. Another group spent the first week of the school year laying on guided tours for the new pupils while yet another provided guides and teas/coffees for their school's parents evenings.

8. Charity events

Rather than just jumping on the back of national events that the school already supports, you could introduce your own projects. The World Vision 24 hour famine (see Appendix) is a great opportunity for you to highlight third-world problems but Tear Fund and Save The Children have other projects that you could support. Or perhaps there are local charities that you could get involved with. You could organise sponsored events but it is better if you can put on a show or activity and charge people to attend... fashion shows, TV Game Shows, challenges, messy games... let your imagination run wild!

9. Outreach events

Why not organise a specifically Christian event for your school or for certain year groups? This could be a lunchtime or evening concert. (Why not try it on Valentine's?) You would need to organise a band, speaker and publicity as well as get permission and sort out such things as stewarding and, if appropriate, costs and refreshments. Local churches can often be helpful in terms of providing much of the above, providing that you give sufficient notice.

10. A school mission

Rather than having just one-off events, some schools host missions where a visiting team will come in for up to a week and take part in lessons and assemblies as well as taking events at lunchtimes and in the evenings. It goes without saying that this needs a lot of careful planning, but having a group of Christians who have experience of sharing their faith in the school context can be extremely positive. They can often use music and drama and are able to present God's good news in ways that pupils can readily identify with.

The above is, of course, just a list of ideas to get *you* thinking. Other groups have done such things as start a gospel singing group, put on plays, and form a Christian band and put on concerts. The important thing is not so much what you do but rather *how you do* what you do. For some, making a stand for their faith will be hard and exposing your group to ridicule could set them back a long way, so make sure that you pray and plan carefully before embarking on any of the more adventurous suggestions. It is far better to do a small thing effectively than to try and overreach yourself and end up with a disaster.

But having said that, do do something! Jesus' disciples did not simply hold mutual support meetings, nor did they spend all their time learning from Jesus' teaching and example. No, he sent them out to get involved with their neighbours and communities (Luke 9:1–6), even though they would undoubtedly have felt as insecure and ill-prepared as you may do. No, they went, did, made mistakes, learnt, went again and eventually managed to launch the worldwide Church! From such humble beginnings, great things are possible.

Chapter seven
Dear Aunt Morag (problem solving)

Dear Morag

I've been running the Christian group here for about a term and a half and to begin with it was fine. We were getting about a dozen pupils from a variety of churches and some with no church connection at all. Then someone suggested that I should invite Pete Johnstone, the youth worker from the local church with the biggest youth group. Don't get me wrong, he was great and he got all his youth group to come too which was also great. But now they seem to have taken over and those who don't go to that church are being made to feel that they're not really a part of it. I tried to talk to Pete about it but he just seemed pleased that his young people were so committed to the group. Well, so am I, but...

Any suggestions?

This is a tricky one! One idea might be to encourage all the group – and Pete – to come along to a meeting where you can really air the issues. A Christian group should not be a second meeting for a church youth group and nor should it be a recruiting ground for one. Help them to understand how the others are feeling and about how they might feel if the situation was reversed. When others are there, try giving some prominence to them and also try to split up into smaller groups so that those from the large group have to get to know some of the others.

Dear Morag

You know that when you blow balloons up for a party they're great for a few days and then after that they just start to look shrivelled and lifeless? Well our Christian group seems to have gone much the same way. At the start of the year we had loads of people coming and there was a real buzz about the place. Now there's just a handful of us still going and we end up doing the same stuff each week.

Please help!

Read Chapters 3 and 4 again! Seriously, this is a situation that almost all groups face at one time or another. It is difficult to sustain everyone's interest week after week, term after term. It might be an idea to try and do some special one-offs such as a *Grill a Christian* event or perhaps to meet in a different place. Some groups have even decided to stop their regular meetings for a few weeks while they spend time praying and chatting about the way forward before relaunching themselves with a new name and a fresh programme.

Dear Morag

Aaaarggh! Our group meets on a Wednesday lunchtime and it's been great... till three weeks ago. Then a group of Year 9 boys started knocking on the window and then running away. Then they started yelling out 'God Squad' and 'Bible Bashers'. Last week they were pulling faces at the door and this week they actually came in (10 minutes late) and giggled and made silly comments all the way through. We don't want to turn them away but they are just SOOO annoying. I've dreamt up a variety of ways of taking revenge, most of them involving small insects and unpleasant rashes but I'm not sure if they're either legal or a good idea.

What do you think?

Again, this is quite a common problem but there are a number of solutions. Firstly, you need to explain to them that they are welcome to the group, providing they arrive on time, stay to the end and agree to abide by certain ground rules regarding their behaviour. If they come but can't be sensible, then you have every right to ban them for a week – or longer if you choose. Finally, if they continue to disrupt, you need to speak to a senior teacher who can support you. Of course, if you can meet in a room where disruption is less likely in the first place (ie on the first floor?), then this could help avoid the problem.

Dear Morag

Every year it's the same. Things are going really well then... Boom! It's the great void. Nothing. Or more to the point no one. It's the exams, of course. Everyone's moaning about how much revision they've got to do and how they haven't got time to come to the group... and then they spend their lunchtimes chatting and doing nothing anyway. Surely they'd be better off coming and praying for inspiration.

What do you think?

Exams affect people in many different ways. Some people find that in between revision they just want to unwind and relax completely while others simply keep to a fairly fixed routine and sort out their revision around everything else that is going on. The important thing is not to make people feel guilty for not coming to the group but rather to let them know that you will be praying for them and that it would be lovely to see them if they *can* come – but that you understand perfectly if they can't. Some groups have actually chosen to stop meeting during exam periods but most continue with a more relaxed programme... chat, share, pray, etc.

Dear Morag

We're thinking of re-naming ourselves as 'The Holy Huddle'. Every week we meet together and talk and pray about how we can get more involved in school life and do some witnessing. But as soon as anyone mentions the possibility of actually doing something, then blind panic sets in and all the excuses about exams, washing your hair, aliens visiting this week, etc start to surface. Is it being completely unrealistic to try to do some serious outreach?

Let me know.

No, but... standing up for God at school may well be one of the most difficult things you will ever choose to do. Being a Christian often isn't the 'in thing' and it can open you up to all sorts of teasing and ridicule. So never come down hard on people who are wrestling with this. On the other hand, God promises that *he* will stand by us and it is important that you do look to share the good news of God in appropriate ways. But if you hope to do this as a group, you will only achieve it by encouraging rather than bullying or playing the guilt card on those who find it difficult.

Dear Morag

Last week, the Head asked to see me. Apparently one of the boys who came to a few of our meetings told his parents that we'd prayed for his Gran (who was ill) and for some reason they got into a strop, wanting to know what sort of group we were and what right had we got to be indoctrinating their son, etc, etc, etc. The Head was really good about it, but I'm still wondering whether we did something wrong.

Did we?

Things like this are actually fairly common and are usually caused by a lack of understanding. The good news is that they are normally sorted out fairly quickly (as seems to be the case with you) once people start talking to each other. It is important to remember, however, that not everything you consider normal at Church will be appropriate for a school meeting – it's a good idea to tread cautiously. You could always send a letter home with any newcomers, explaining the aims and practices of the group but, if in doubt, talk the situation over with those who are taking the responsibility for the group.

Dear Morag

As part of our programme at Christmas we put on a special outreach meeting in the Hall at lunchtime. We had games, a band and one of the local youth workers gave a talk. It was really excellent – loads of people came – and afterwards two Year 9 pupils went up to the youth worker, saying that they wanted to become Christians. He asked me to join them the next day when he went through a booklet and prayed with them. But he can't come in every week and they don't live near his church.

What do I do?

Firstly, praise God! It's brilliant that you were able to put on an event like that and that you got such a good response. Secondly, don't panic! You don't need to feel that you alone are responsible for their follow-up. God may have other means of support for them. It would, however, be good to encourage them to come along to the group, and do try to find out if there are other churches nearer to their home where they could be cared for. It may be that you will need to fix up an initial meeting or even go along with them to a service. Even if you're not in a position to do either of these, then at least pray that God will provide the support they need through others.

Dear Morag

We've got a really good group with a real cross-section of ages and church backgrounds. At least, I thought that would be a good thing. The difficulty is that when we have times of prayer, some of them want to speak in tongues while there are others – myself included – who really aren't comfortable with that. The only solution seems to be not to pray at all, but if a Christian group can't pray, what can it do?

Your thoughts?

This kind of thing can always be an issue when you bring together groups from a range of denominations and church backgrounds. While I would certainly not want to stop young people from exercising their gifts, I would suggest that you ask them whether they are using them wisely in this case. It is likely that the school would not be happy with the exercising of the more supernatural gifts but, more to the point, if their action is a stumbling block that may stop others coming to the meeting, then they should be challenged to put the unity of the whole Christian body in school first and save their gifts for a more appropriate setting.

Section B

For the following outlines,
we have assumed that you have access to:

pens
paper
Blu-tack
a Bible
a black/white board or OHP
chairs and tables

Where other items are required, these are
specified at the start of each outline. We do
strongly recommend, however, that you read
carefully through each one well in advance of
your meeting so that you are fully prepared for
each activity.

1 Who is God?

Aim:

To provide the young people with the opportunity to consider some different characteristics of God. You will need: flip chart

Tuning in
(10 mins):

Ask the young people to sit beside someone that they know very well. Explain that you will choose two sets of partners. One partner from each pair will leave the room while the other two will be asked questions about their friends.

After one from each pair has left the room, ask the remaining two to answer as accurately as possible:

1   What is your partner's favourite colour?
2   What is your partner's favourite sport?
3   What did they do last night?
4   What did they have for breakfast?
5   Add some more of your own questions.

Bring the partners back into the room and ask them the same questions. Which set of partners knew each other the best? Talk about how much we may know about each other and compare this to how much we may know about God.

Play
(15 mins):

What do we really know about God? Brainstorm ideas and make a note on a flip chart. Tell the group that together you are going to discover a little of what God is like. Ask them to work with their partner. Give each pair a sheet of A4 paper. Ask them to fold it in half, in half again and then in half again. When unfolded, there should be eight boxes.

Tell them that around the room are verses from the Bible that tell us a bit about who God is and what he has done (see verses on the next page). Ask them to draw what the verse tells them about God (eg for the verse on creation, draw a small picture about God creating the world). If they really can't think what to draw, they can write the verse down. Set them the task of completing as many as they can in the allocated time.

Verses to use:

(The words in bold are the answers.)

1 'God is exalted in his power. Who is **a teacher** like him?' (Job 36:22)

2 'I the Lord **do not change**...' (Malachi 3:6)

3 'Oh Lord, you have searched me and **you know me**. You know when I sit and when I rise; you perceive my thoughts from afar.' (Psalm 139:1,2)

4 'In the beginning **God created the heavens and the earth**.' (Genesis 1:1)

5 '**A faithful God** who does no wrong, upright and just is he.' (Deuteronomy 32:4)

6 'Whoever does not love does not know God because **God is love**.' (1 John 4:8)

7 'The Lord is **my helper**; I will not be afraid.' (Hebrews 13:6)

8 'The Lord is **my shepherd** I shall not be in want.' (Psalm 23:1)

9 'God is our **refuge and strength**, an ever present help in trouble.' (Psalm 46:1)

10 'I will give thanks to the Lord because of **his righteousness**...' (Psalm 7:17)

Pause

(10 mins):

Ask them to show their pictures and talk about what they discovered about God. Was there anything they knew already? What did they most like about God? What was their favourite verse? Finish by talking about what is important to you about God and why.

Fast forward

(10 mins):

In larger groups make a poster, cutting out the pictures from the *Play* activity showing what God is like.

2 Jesus - who?

Aim:

To help the young people to understand the person of Jesus and his deity.

You will need: sticky labels.

Tuning in
(10 mins):

Have a list of names (one for each person there) of famous people written on sticky labels. (They could be alive or dead, cartoon or real, human or animal. Examples could include Prince Charles, Asterix, Glenn Hoddle, Shakespeare, Tony Blair, Superman, etc.) Attach a label to each person's back. Tell the group that they are to find out who they are (the name written on their back). They are to do this by asking questions of the others in the room, eg 'Am I a human?' 'Am I alive?' etc. The only answers that can be given are 'Yes' or 'No'. As they ask questions, they will also answer those who ask them questions. Once they have guessed who they are, they can either sit down or get another label (assuming you have some spares.)

Play
(15 mins):

Start by explaining to the young people that, as a group, they are going to consider who Jesus is. Remind them that they discovered who they were in the game by asking questions. How might they find out who Jesus is? What questions would they ask?

Split the group into pairs. Tell them they are now going to go around the room and find passages from the Bible that talk about Jesus. Give each pair a sheet of A4 paper folded in half. Ask them to write at the top of the left-hand side of the page 'LIKE US' and on the right 'NOT LIKE US'. Tell them they have to read the passage and decide whether what Jesus did was like us or not. They then write what Jesus did on the appropriate side of the page.

'When Mary reached the place where Jesus was and saw him, she fell at his feet and said, "Lord, if you had been here, my brother would not have died." ... **Jesus wept**.' (John 11:32,35)

'On the third day a wedding took place at Cana in Galilee ... **Jesus and his disciples had also been invited to the wedding**.' (John 2:1,2)

'Without warning, a furious storm came up on the lake, so that the waves swept over the boat. But **Jesus was sleeping**.' (Matthew 8:24)

'During the fourth watch of the night Jesus went out to them, **walking on the lake**.' (Matthew 14:25)

'The disciples went and woke him, saying, "Master, Master, we're going to drown!" **He [Jesus] got up and rebuked the wind** and the raging waters; the storm subsided, **and all was calm**.' (Luke 8:24)

'When Jesus had finished speaking, a Pharisee invited him to **eat with him**; so he went in and reclined at the table.' (Luke 11:37)

'Jesus, **tired** as he was from the journey, sat down by the well. It was about the sixth hour.' (John 4:6)

'"What do you want me to do for you?" Jesus asked him.

The blind man said, "Rabbi, I want to see." "Go," said Jesus, "your faith has healed you." **Immediately he received his sight** and followed Jesus along the road.' (Mark 10:51,52)

'... people brought to him all who were ill with various diseases, those suffering severe pain, the demon-possessed, those having seizures and the paralysed, and **he healed them**.' (Matthew 4:24)

'Jesus went with his disciples to a place called Gethsemane and he said to them, **"Sit here while I go over there and pray."**' (Matthew 26:36)

Pause
(10 mins):
Find out what they have put on which page. Talk a bit about how Jesus was both like and yet not like us.

God and Man – Read Matthew 1:23. Briefly talk about how God sent Jesus who was truly God and yet came to us as a man.

Fast forward
(10 mins):
Split into small groups. Give them large sheets of paper and colouring pens. Ask them to make a poster titled 'JESUS, MORE THAN A MAN'.

Following Jesus ③

Aim:

To look at how Jesus chose ordinary people to follow him.

You will need: appropriate gear for *The Amazon Adventure.*

Tuning in

(10 mins):
The Amazon adventure

(This works best if you come in with the lights off, dressed appropriately for an adventure.) Tell the group that you are going on an adventure, a dangerous one. You are going to the Amazon jungle. Briefly describe the dangers involved, such as wild animals, swamps, diseases, etc. Go on to say that you need some volunteers to come with you. They need to be brave and strong to protect you. You are looking for the best, smartest, fittest, etc. In order to find out who these people are, you have devised a test. Select some volunteers to do the following test, eliminating people as you go along. (If you have an older group it is easy to adjust the scene to make it more sophisticated. For example, you could ask the group what type of person you would look for to go on such an adventure.)

The test has two parts to it – a mental test and a physical test. Both are intended to be a fun way of showing how we would find out who was best to go.

Mental test (These are trick questions. Answers in brackets.)

1　Mississippi is a difficult word to spell. Spell it.
　(IT.)
2　How far can a man run into the woods?
　(Halfway.)
3　Some months have 30 days, some have 31, but how many have 28?
　(All of them.)
4　How many animals of each species did Moses take into the ark?
　(None – Noah built the ark, not Moses.)
5　What would you find in the middle of Toronto?
　(O.)
6　If I had 2 coins in my hand totalling 55p and one is not a 50p, what are the 2 coins?
　(50p and 5p. The other is a 50p.)
7　Why can't a man living to the north of the Thames be buried in south London?
　(He is still living.)
8　How much dirt is in a 3 foot by 3 foot hole?
　(None – it's a hole.)

Physical test

1　An arm wrestle.
2　A tug of war.
3　Any others you can think of.

Finish this section by not choosing anyone. Go on to say how your life is too important to put in their hands.

Play

(20 mins):

Talk about Jesus having to find a team of people to help him. Go on to mention that Jesus is a lot more important than any of us. Who do they think he would have chosen to help him? To a degree, Jesus was trusting the gospel message into their hands. Tell the group that together you are going to look at three of the people Jesus chose. (Don't forget to mention that there were others he chose as well.) The three people we are going to look at are Peter, Matthew and James.

Disciple hunt: Split the pupils into small groups. Give them each a sheet of paper and pen. Have the following verses about the disciples spread around the room. Ask:

1 What was the occupation of a) Peter
   b) Matthew c) James?
2 Where was Peter from?
3 Do we know of any brothers and sisters
   Peter had?

(You may wish to have duplicate copies of the following verses to avoid crowding round.)

Peter *'As Jesus walked beside the Sea of Galilee, he saw Simon [Peter] and his brother Andrew casting a net into the lake, for they were fishermen.' (Mark 1:16)*

Matthew *'As Jesus went on from there, he saw a man named Matthew sitting at the tax collector's booth.' (Matthew 9:9)*

Peter *'These are the names of the twelve apostles: first, Simon (who is called Peter) and his brother Andrew.' (Matthew 10:2)*

James *'... he saw two other brothers, James son of Zebedee and his brother John. They were in a boat with their father Zebedee, preparing their nets.' (Matthew 4:21)*

Peter *'Philip, like Andrew and Peter, was from the town of Bethsaida.' (John 1:44)*

Bring the group together and find out what they have discovered. Talk about how Jesus chose people like Peter, Andrew and James who were ordinary people with ordinary jobs (eg fishermen). Matthew, who was a tax collector, wasn't even very popular but Jesus chose him anyway. Explain that Jesus is interested in us regardless of how smart, fit or popular we are.

Pause

(15 mins):

Split the pupils into slightly bigger groups.

Read Matthew 4:18–22 (the calling of the first disciples). Tell the group this is how Jesus called Peter and James. What an adventure they were about to have! Give the groups a large sheet of paper and pens. Ask them to quickly write down as many things they can think of that Jesus did while he was on earth eg the miracles, teachings, etc.

After a while, get some feedback. Bring out that the disciples were embarking on a fantastic adventure. Yet, at this stage, these things hadn't happened. How might they have felt? Go through the following possible reactions *(showing the relevant picture for each on page ●●●).*

Who me? (I'm only a fisherman.)
Fear/timidity (What will happen?)
Scared (They may have been a little scared.)
Eager (Keen to get started. Jesus had impressed them.)
Excitement (They might have felt they couldn't wait to see what was going to happen.)

Fast forward

(5 mins):

They were about to go on a great adventure. What would have happened if Jesus had asked them to follow him and they had said 'no' because they were too busy or they didn't want to? They would have missed out on the best life they could have had – not necessarily an easy life but certainly a very exciting one.

Finish this bit off by mentioning that Jesus also wants us to follow him today.

27

4 Servant Jesus

Aim:

To allow the young people to appreciate that Jesus came to serve.

You will need: *The Challenger: The Champion* video (SU, optional).

Tuning in (10 mins):

Start off by splitting the pupils into groups. Ask them to sit in circles around the room. On a desk at the front make separate piles of A5 pieces of paper with one letter of each of the following letters on a sheet: V S A N E T O R D P. Ensure that you have a separate pile for each group.

Tell them you are going to ask them a question with a one word answer. From the answer you are looking for the first letter. Having worked out the first letter they then need to run out to where their set of letters are, collect the letter they are looking for and bring it back to the group. A point is given to the group that brings the correct letter back to their group first. After collecting all the letters they have to then unscramble them to work out the word SERVANT. The letters O D P are just spare ones.

Jumble up the order of the questions.

A star that gives us heat	Sun
The capital of Scotland	Edinburgh
The opposite of wrong	Right
The fifth last letter of the alphabet	V
Neil Armstong was an — — — —	Astronaut
The 14th letter of the alphabet	N
What is always coming but never comes	Tomorrow

Briefly discuss what a servant is. Ask them who would employ a servant. People who were very wealthy and important had servants.

Play (20 mins):

Tell the group that Jesus was a very important person who was once described as the King of Kings. You would have expected him to have servants yet this was not the case. Jesus actually served other people. Ask them to think of ways that Jesus served people. In the same groups as before, give out one of the following passages. As a group they have to act it out for others to see how Jesus served other people.

Healing of two blind men (Matthew 20:29–34)

'As Jesus and his disciples were leaving Jericho, a large crowd followed him. Two blind men were sitting by the roadside, and when they heard that Jesus was going by, they shouted, "Lord, Son of David, have mercy on us!" The crowd rebuked them and told them to be quiet, but they shouted all the louder, "Lord, Son of David, have mercy on us!" Jesus stopped and called them. "What do you want me to do for you?" he asked. "Lord," they answered, "we want our sight." Jesus had compassion on them and touched their eyes. Immediately they received their sight and followed him.'

Healing of deaf men (Mark 7:31–37)

'Then Jesus left the vicinity of Tyre and went through Sidon, down to the Sea of Galilee and into the region of the Decapolis. There some people brought to him a man who was deaf and could hardly talk, and they begged him to place his hand on the man. After he took him aside, away from the crowd, Jesus put his fingers into the man's ears. Then he spat and touched the man's tongue. He looked up to heaven and with a deep sigh said to him, *Ephphatha!*" (which means, "Be opened!"). At this, the man's ears were opened, his tongue was loosened and he began to speak plainly. Jesus commanded them not to tell anyone. But the more he did so, the more they kept talking about it. People were overwhelmed with amazement. "He has done everything well," they said. "He even makes the deaf hear and the mute speak."'

Feeding of 5,000 (Matthew 14:17–20)

'"We have here only five loaves of bread and two fish," they answered. "Bring them here to me," he said. And he directed the people to sit down on the grass. Taking the five loaves and the two fish and looking up to heaven, he gave thanks and broke the loaves. Then he gave them to the disciples, and the disciples gave them to the people. They all ate and were satisfied, and the disciples picked up twelve baskets full of broken pieces that were left over.'

Washing of the disciple's feet (John 13:4–7)

'So he got up from the meal, took off his outer clothing, and wrapped a towel around his waist. After that, he poured water into a basin and began to wash his disciples' feet, drying them with the towel that was wrapped around him. He came to Simon Peter, who said to him, "Lord, are you going to wash my feet?" Jesus replied, "You do not realise now what I am doing, but later you will understand."'

Pause
(10 mins):
Talk about the ways Jesus did things for others. Ask why he did them. Bring out his love, care, etc. Read Matthew 20:28: 'Just as the Son of Man did not come to be served but to serve, and to give his life as a ransom for many.' Re-emphasise the point that you would expect Jesus to have people running after him but in fact he came to serve.

Fast forward
(5 mins):
Drama takes up a lot of time so there probably won't be time for another activity. If there is, you may wish to show the video *The Challenger: The Champion* (SU). Episode one, Palm Sunday, shows Jesus entering Jerusalem riding on a donkey. Bring out how, although he could have had an army of angels to accompany him, he chose to come on a mere donkey.

What is sin? outline 5

Aim:

To help the young people to consider a) how sin started and b) how sin separates us from God.
You will need: Play-doh, pictures from 106 and 107.

Tuning in
(10 mins):

Split the group into smaller groups. Give each group a pile of scrap paper or some Play-doh. Ask them to consider the world and everything in it. What is special to them? Ask them to make a model/cut-out of this object using the Play-doh or paper. Go round the groups complimenting them on their masterpieces.

Bring out something you have made and talk about why it is really special to you. Mention the time, care and attention you put into making it. Explain that when God made the earth he was really pleased with everything that he made but, out of it all, the best thing he made was mankind. He created us to have a relationship with him and he enjoys our friendship.

Play
(10 mins):

From the following pictures of a tree, an apple and two people, go through the story of how sin entered the world.

People: God created Adam and Eve. He really enjoyed the friendship with them.

Tree: God put them in a beautiful place with lots to eat. There was one tree they were not to eat from.

Apple: Its fruit looked good but they were not to eat from it.

People: But Adam and Eve did eat from it, even though God had told them not to. They sinned against God.

Show a glass of clear water. Mention to the group that this is how God created people: perfect in every way. There was nothing wrong with them. But when Adam and Eve ate the fruit it was all spoilt. Add some food colouring to the water (purple or a dark colour works best). Say that sin came into the world and affected everything, including us. The world was spoilt and we now had sin in our lives. No matter how good we think we are, human nature is now sinful, bad and corrupt. So right from the word 'go' we are sinful. You may see this when you look at a baby or a child: you don't need to teach it how to be naughty. It comes naturally!

The gulf: Tell the group that because of our sinful nature we have moved away from God. He cannot be in the presence of sin. This has resulted in us being separated from God. There is a gulf we can not get over. Illustrate the gulf by showing the picture below of two cliffs opposite each other. God is on one side and we are on the other (this is a popular illustration but very effective at getting the point across). In the middle of the two cliffs is written 'sinful nature'. This picture could also be illustrated using volunteers – one for each side of the cliff. One volunteer tries to reach the other by jumping over the gap, which of course is impossible. End this section by emphasising that we now can't get to God by ourselves.

⏸ Pause:
(10 mins):
Talk about how God feels about the way we have spoilt our relationship with him. Read Genesis 6:5: 'The LORD saw how great man's wickedness on the earth had become, and that every inclination of the thoughts of his heart was only evil all the time. The LORD was grieved that he had made man on the earth, and his heart was filled with pain.'

The result of having a sinful nature is that we are now naturally drawn to doing wrong and we hurt and anger God as we distance ourselves from him, acting destructively towards others and the world around us. God sees this and is desperately upset.

Give each group a large sheet of paper and ask them to write in the middle of the page 'We hurt and anger God when we …'. Then ask them to brainstorm as many things as they can think of that we do wrong. Point out how these things hurt God and that we are all guilty for pushing God away and spoiling the relationship with God. We spoil the perfect world God made, by the things we do. Ask the group how they would feel if you jumped on their masterpieces, especially if they had spent hours perfecting them.

⏩ Fast forward:
(10 mins):
Conclude by talking about how hurt God is that his relationship with us is spoilt, along with the world he created so perfectly. Yet God did not give up on us. He still loves us and next week we will see what God did about it.

The cross

Aim:

To help the young people fully appreciate that Jesus' death on the cross is the only way in which we can have a friendship with God.

You will need: *Jesus of Nazareth* video (optional).

Tuning in

(10 mins):

Start off by asking what the following have in common: A goal keeper, a stamp collector and an ambulance man.

The answer is, they all have the word *save* in common. Go on to mention how we are going to look at how Jesus saved us! From what?

Matching pairs

Play matching pairs, having the following situations and people written on pieces of paper (one on each). Give each pupil a piece of paper. (If there is an odd number of young people you will need to join in too.) They have to go around saying who or what they are. This will either be the person in trouble or the rescue service. Once they have found the correct partner they are to sit down. *(You could play a few times before moving on to the next section. Think of some other examples or just duplicate the situations here.)*

PERSON	RESCUE SERVICE
You are trapped under the snow on a mountain	Mountain rescue team
Your car has just broken down	AA (road help)
Your boat is sinking	The lifeboat
Your house is on fire	The fire brigade
You are being mugged	The police

Afterwards finish by talking about the fact that the person knew that they needed help and they also knew who they needed it from.

Play

(15 mins):

Tell the group we are going to look at how Jesus was the best rescue service of all. Recap on last week's session on sin. Tell them that the result of sin coming into the world was separation from God. Death came with Adam and Eve disobeying God. We would now all one day die.

Using the same illustration as last week, show the gap between us and God. Use volunteers to show the picture of the cliffs. Have one volunteer being each cliff, standing opposite each other with a large gap in the middle. Tell the group to imagine that the drop between the cliff doesn't end where the floor does, but goes so deep that we are unable to see the bottom. Using a third volunteer standing on the 'US' cliff talk about how we (humans) have tried to get back to God. We have tried several ways. Use the words below to describe ways we have tried to bridge the gap with, and get back to God:

Doing good things/go to church/pray

(Make up more of your own suitable for your group.)
This works well if you have each word written on paper that looks like or has a bridge drawn on it. The bridges can be of various lengths but none should come anywhere near the other cliff.
The trouble is, no matter how hard we try we can't get our relationship right with God. Only God can.

Pause:
(15 mins):
Show the *Jesus of Nazareth* video and/or read Mark 15:6-15. If you show the video then select a relevant bit showing Jesus' death. You will need to conclude by either reading or telling them about Jesus' resurrection.

After the video, talk about how the only way that Jesus could save us so that we could have a friendship with God, was by dying on the cross. He did it for us. Go on to read Mark 16:1-6.

Talk about how Jesus rose from the dead. God knew we could not get close to him and that only he could do something about it. So God sent Jesus. Only Jesus could bridge the gap between us and God because he had no sin in his life. Being God, he did not have a sinful nature as we have.

Tell the story of a boy called Ian who was caught stealing at school. It was in the days when beating someone with a belt was allowed as a punishment. The teacher pulled the belt out of the drawer. Tom, a good friend of Ian's, knowing that Ian was about to get belted and possibly even expelled for getting into trouble for the last time, stood up. Although Tom hadn't done anything wrong, he said that he had stolen the stuff. He walked to the front and took the punishment

instead of Ian. (You may wish to make up a similar story. True ones are better.)

Jesus did not take the belt for us but he did die for us. He took on himself all the wrong things we do as a result of our sinful nature and died on a cross for us, taking the punishment that should have been ours. He did not have to but because God loves us, and he knew it was the only way to help us, he did it. Reiterate how only Jesus could have done this because he was the only perfect, sinless man to have lived.

Using the picture of the cliff from last week, show the deep gulf between us and God. Remind them that *we* could not bridge the gap but that *God* did. While saying this, draw a picture of a cross bridging the gap between both cliffs.

Fast forward
(10 mins):
Party illustration

Show the group an invitation you received to a party (make up a simple invitation, making sure that you write 'RSVP' in the corner). Talk about how special you feel at being invited, how you are looking forward to the party, etc. Say you have the invitation but it requires you to do something about it. Ask for suggestions as to what you should do. After a while someone will probably point out the RSVP. Say that it is no good having the invitation unless you reply. You need to do something about it.

Jesus did this for each one of us. What is our response? Each one of us can now be in right relationship with God again but we need to do something about it. We need to ask Jesus to forgive us and follow him. (This last bit you will need to do carefully depending on your group and how much they have understood.) End by asking the group if they have any questions and suggest that, if they want to know more, they can come and see you after the meeting.

The Holy Spirit

outline **7**

Aim:

To provide the young people with the opportunity to discover who the Holy Spirit is and what he does.

NB. It's important to remember that as human beings we are never fully going to understand God, so no illustration or explanation of The Trinity is ever going to be truly satisfactory. So much about God is a profound mystery to us, reminding us how limited our human minds are compared to God's.

Tuning in:
(10 mins):
Silly sum games

Start off by seeing who can work out the following sums mentally, the quickest.

    9X9 =   81

    (1+12)X3 =   39

Make up some of your own but finish with the next couple of trick questions:

    12X2X4X6X12X0= 0

    1X1X1=   1

Comment how the last sum is a confusing one, where we can multiply three numbers together yet have the same number as the answer.

The Trinity:

Tell the group that you are going to think about the Holy Spirit. 'Who is he?' you might ask. Well, he is God. Go on to explain there is only one God but that he exists as God the Father, God the Son (Jesus) and God the Holy Spirit. The three together are God. Each one is not just a part of God but is God.

This is a difficult concept to grasp. Show the group a tube of Aqua toothpaste and squirt a little onto a piece of paper. Comment on the fact that it is one tube of toothpaste yet three colours have come out of the tube. Each colour has a different function to play: red - for plaque, blue - for breath, white - to clean teeth.

It's not three different tubes of toothpaste, but one. You may need to remind the group, however, that this is only a very limited illustration of The Trinity. We will never understand everything about God – after all, that's what makes him God! We know a bit about God the Father and God the Son, but now we are going to find out about God the Spirit (or the Holy Spirit).

Play:
(15 mins):

Split the group into three. Give each small group one of the following passages and tell them that before Jesus died he told us about the Holy Spirit who would be coming to help us. We are going to act out how the Holy Spirit first came. Being God, he has always been here, but we're talking about when he specifically came to help us after Jesus died and went to be with his Father. Go on to tell the young people that, in their groups, they are going to act out their bit of the story in turn so that everyone can see what happened.

Group 1 John 14:16,17

Act out Jesus telling the disciples about the

Holy Spirit coming. Think about the disciples' reactions. Questions they might ask include: Who is he? What is he like? What will he do? How will he help?, etc.

Group 2 Acts 2:1–4

Act out the Holy Spirit coming and the disciples' reaction.

Group 3 Acts 2:12–17

Act out some people being confused; other people making fun of Jesus' friends and then finally Peter standing up to say that what has happened is from God.

Pause

(10 mins):

A close friend

Split them into small groups. Give each group a large sheet of paper and pens and ask them to draw an outline of a person. Then ask them to write around the side of the person things that make a good friend (sense of humour, similar interests, etc). Talk about how the Holy Spirit is like a close friend who helps and supports us.

Mention the following three things about the Holy Spirit and ask them to vote on which one they think is the most important to them.

1 **He protects us:** He is there when things are difficult and tough, protecting us from things that will harm us.

2 **He is always there:** Wherever we go he is there. In every situation we go through, he is there with us.

3 **He guides and helps us:** He shows us the right way to live. He helps us when things get tough and hard.

Expand on the different points, bringing out how the Holy Spirit is a good friend. Go on to mention that also, because he is a close friend, he has feelings and bring out the following points.

1 Being God he is a person not an 'it'. John 16:7-15

2 We can upset him. The Bible calls it grieving the Holy Spirit. Ephesians 4:30

3 We can please him.

Fast forward

(10 mins):

So we have seen how the Holy Spirit is God and how he can be described as a close friend, but what does he do? We have mentioned already his function is to help us, but how does he do this?

Match the verse:

Play match the verse by giving each group a copy of the following words written on separate pieces of paper.

Lives in Christians – Romans 8:9

Speaks – Acts 13:2

Prays with us – Romans 8:26

Leads / directs – Acts 8:29

Commands, tells us what to do – Acts 16:6,7

Gives gifts to his people – Romans 12:1–8; 1 Corinthians 12 and 14.

Teaches – John 14:26

Reminds – John 14:26

Convicts – John 16:8–11

Gives us power – Acts 1:8

Changes our lives for the better – Galatians 5:16,22,23

Read the following passages one at a time. See if they can work out which word describes the Holy Spirit from the verse. Spend a short amount of time explaining each one. To make this more of a game, give points to the first group who runs out to you with the correct word for the verse.

Romans 8:9 Acts 13:2 Romans 8:26 Acts 8:29 Acts 16:6,7

Tell the groups you are looking for two words from the next verse.

John 14:26 John 16:8-11 Acts 1:8

Conclude by saying how great and wonderful God is.

8 Prayer

Aim:

To look at what prayer is and why we should pray.

You will need: *Blu-tack, paper.*

Tuning in

(10 mins):

Play hangman to guess the word COMMUNICATION. Ask the group to tell you what it means. From the list below scramble up the letters, making anagrams of each word. Write each one separately on a piece of paper and spread the words around the room. Ask everyone to find a partner. Tell them that they have to go around unscrambling the letters to make the correct word, until they have all the words. Don't forget to tell them that all the words have something to do with communication.

TELEGRAM
MORSE CODE
TELEPHONE
TELEVISION
MESSENGER
RADIO
FAX
LETTER
E-MAIL

Play

(10 mins):

BT had the slogan 'It's good to talk.' Why is it good to talk? Bring out the importance of communicating. How do we communicate with God? Through prayer.

Ask the group if they have ever prayed to God. Mention how most people at some times in their lives have prayed to God.

Discuss the following questions:

1 What sort of people pray?
2 Where is it best to pray?
3 What things should we pray about?
4 How often should we pray?
5 Does God listen when we pray?
6 Does God do anything about what we pray about?

Briefly finish this section by talking about how God likes it when we pray.

Also bring out that prayer should not be one long shopping list. This could be illustrated by telling the story of Bob who, whenever he sees his friend, Ian, says something along the lines of 'Hello Ian, I could really do with a new bike. By the way, I have a test tomorrow. Could you help me with it? And, of course, I need some more money. How about lending me your new Rollerblades? Oh, and you know how you were thinking of buying me that new Nike top? Well I think it's a good idea...' He is only friends with Ian for what he can get from him.

God likes it when we talk to him, thanking him for who he is and for what he has done for us.

⏸ Pause

(15 mins):

Use the simple description of traffic lights to describe prayer (you may have come across this before). When we pray God always answers us. It may not, however, be the answer we are looking for. God's answers could be described a bit like a set of traffic lights:

Red: God says no. God always knows best. Sometimes it is hard and we don't understand why. We may never understand but we do need to trust God. (It is worth backing this up with a personal experience of this, if you have one.)
Amber: God says wait. It may not be the right time or God may be wanting to teach/show you something.
Green: God says yes. The answer we like best. He gives us what we ask for.
(If you have time you may want to draw the lights to emphasise the points.) Mention how God knows all about us and wants the best for us.

What is the answer?

There are times when you may pray and never hear an answer. Ask the group if they still think God has heard the prayer. Briefly talk about how God hears all our prayers and answers them. There are times when we may not understand the answer or when God does not appear to show us the answer, but there is no doubt that he has heard our prayer. His answer may have been for us not to know.

It isn't always easy trusting someone. But God is someone whom we can trust. He wants the best for us and he won't let us down.

Two way communication

Ask for a couple of volunteers. Give them the following scenarios to act out:

1 A person giving a deaf lady instruction on how to get to the shops.
2 A person asking a friend to help him with his homework, but the friend is too busy talking for them to get a word in edgeways.

Ask the group if they have ever felt that no one is listening to them. Do they sometimes wonder if God feels like that? Often, we are so busy *talking* to him, asking for things we want, that we don't spend any time *listening*. Mention that prayer should be a two-way communication between us and God.

⏩ Fast forward

(10 mins):

Read 1 Timothy 2:1: 'I urge then, first of all, that requests, prayers, intercession and thanksgiving be made for everyone.' Ask the group what things we should pray for.

Split them into smaller groups and give each group small pieces of paper and pens. At the front of the room have a large piece of paper and some Blu-tack. (If you have time, it would be worthwhile making the large piece of paper look like a wall and the pieces of paper like bricks.) Ask the groups to write down things that they may want prayer for, both personal and wider issues. Tell them that after they have written them down, they should bring them to the front and stick them on the prayer wall. Ask them to keep doing this until you have a good number on the wall. It is also worthwhile asking them to really think through what they are writing. Finish by praying for the things that are written down.

The Bible

outline 9

Aim:

To look at the importance of reading the Bible.

You will need: the *How to Beat the System* video (SU, optional); a briefcase/bag; a candle and matches (optional).

Tuning in
(10 mins):

Start off by entering the room acting suspiciously, carrying a briefcase or bag. In a quiet voice tell the group you have something hidden in it. Can they guess what it is? Go on to say that what is hidden in your briefcase has been smuggled into many countries. People have died for smuggling it. Some people have even been killed for using it. It has changed people's lives. Can anyone guess what it is now?

Open the briefcase to show a pile of papers at the top which are hiding several Bibles underneath. Tell the group that you have more than one of the objects in the briefcase. Any last guesses? Take out the papers to reveal the Bibles underneath.

Tell the true story of how a lorry, full of medical aid, food and some Bibles went to Romania. While the lorry was being unloaded, there was a greater interest in the Bibles than in the food or medical help. The Romanians were climbing over each other to get one! Why were they so keen to get the Bibles, you may ask? For several years, in communist Romania, the Bible had been forbidden. You were not allowed to have one and

if you were caught with one you were in trouble. Yet the desire of many people to have one was still there. With the fall of communism came a change in the law. You were now allowed to have a Bible but they were very scarce and people were so keen to have them. The trouble is that often, in this country, we take the Bible's availability for granted.

Play
(10 mins):

Do the following quiz about the Bible. Label each corner of the room A, B, C, or D. Tell the group that they have to stand by the letter they think is the correct answer to the following questions:

1 How many books are in the Old Testament?
   a) 33 b) 35 **c) 39** d) 42
2 How many books are in the New Testament?
   a) 22 **b) 27** c) 32 d) 37
3 The Bible is a collection of books
   a) true b) false
4 The Bible was written by many different people.
   a) true b) false
5 The Bible was written over about 500 years.
   a) true **b) false – 1000+ years**

Ask each member of the group to find a partner. Ask one of each pair to close their eyes. (This activity actually works better if you use blindfolds.) Their partner then has to guide them around the room, avoiding desks, chairs or any other objects that may be in the way. This is done by either holding their shoulder and guiding them or by speaking directions into their ear. After a while get partners to swap roles, then ask the pairs to open their eyes/take off the blindfolds and form small groups.

Pause
(15 mins):

Read Psalm 119:105: 'Your word is a lamp to my feet and a light for my path.' It is worthwhile lighting a candle at this point as a visual aid. Give out a large sheet of paper and pens to the groups. Ask them to write down how the Bible helps us. (They may need a bit of help but this is best assessed when going round the groups.) Ideas to feed in include: how the Bible directs us, how it shows us the right way to live and what to avoid, etc.

Give the following list to the group. Tell them that this is why we have the Bible. Ask them if they want to add any more to it. Then ask them to number the things the Bible does in order of importance.

★ *Guides us*
★ *Helps us to get to know more about God and Jesus*
★ *Shows us the best way to live*
★ *Teaches us about the history of the world*
★ *Warns us of things we should do or not do*
★ *Helps us to be wise*

Finish this section by bringing out that the Bible does all these things but that the most important thing the Bible teaches us is how we can get to know God personally.

Fast forward
(10 mins):

Ask everyone to get into pairs. Give each pair a piece of paper and pen and tell them they are going to learn from two passages in the Bible: 2 Timothy 3:16,17 and Romans 15:4. These passages tell us what the Bible is used for. Tell them they have five minutes in which to find the slips of paper hidden around the room showing what the passages have to say.

On the slips of paper hidden around the room write the following:
Given by God
Teaches the truth
Tells us off
Corrects us
Shows us right way to live
Gives hope

Tell them about your favourite book in the Bible and explain why you chose that particular one. Finish by mentioning the many Bible reading notes that are available. (It would be good if you could bring along some sample copies to show/give out. Contact Scripture Union Sales and Promotions for free samples of *One Up* (11–14 year olds) and *Disclosure* (14–25 year olds).
Note: There is a good video called *How to Beat the System* (SU, see Appendix). It is all about the Bible, is fun to watch and would be well worth showing to your group.

Fellowship and growth

outline
10

Aim:

To look at the function of the church and how we should grow.

You will need: pictures (see *Pause*).

Tuning in
(10 mins):

On Sunday, I... Play a game in which everyone sits in a circle. The first person starts off by saying something like, 'On Sunday I washed my car.' The second person then repeats what the first person said and adds their own idea, eg 'I went to a car boot sale.' Continue round the circle, adding things that people tend to do on Sundays. Play for a few minutes and then introduce (refer back if it's already been mentioned in the game) the idea of going to church. Emphasise that, for Christians, this is often a vital part of every Sunday.

Why go to church?

Split the pupils into smaller groups and give each group a large sheet of paper and pens. Ask them to draw a picture of a church. Then, inside or around it, ask them to write down five reasons why people choose to go to church. Have a time for feedback and then emphasise the following reasons:

★ *To worship God.*
★ *To learn more about God and how to follow Jesus.*

★ *To hear the Bible read and explained.*
★ *For fellowship: to meet with other people who have the same aims and who can encourage and support each other through the ups and downs of Christian life.*

Play
(15 mins):

Ask the groups why they think people who follow Jesus go to church. After you have exhausted their suggestions play the **Auction game**. Tell the groups they each have £100 to spend or bid on different reasons why people who follow Jesus go to church and that each reason has a value, which you will only reveal at the end of all the bidding.

As you go through the list, spend time commenting on how each reason benefits someone who follows Jesus. Ask the groups to think among themselves how much each is worth. Remind them you won't tell them the value until after all the bidding is done, but they need to decide now which they think is worth putting more money on.

1 Friends who understand you. (Those who also follow Jesus will understand what you are going through.)

2 Friends who will help you. (Other Christians are there who will help you when things get tough.)

3 Friends to share things with. (Other Christians are there who have things in common with you.)

4 Friends who will teach you. (There will be people who are a bit further

down the road in their faith than you, who can encourage, challenge and teach you more about who God is.)

5   Friends who will protect you. (There will be Christians there who will watch out for you.)

6   Friends who you can have a laugh with. (You'll meet people there who enjoy the same things as you.)

After you have gone through the items on the list have fun auctioning them. The key here is not to take it too seriously. After the last bid is finalised by the hammer, deduct the amount they bid from the £100 they have to spend. Keep a record of how much each group has left to spend, watching out for any who go over their limit.

Finally tell the groups you are now going to reveal the true value for each item so they can see if they bid wisely. After a build up, go on to say that you can't actually put a value on them. At different times some reasons will be more important than others. There are times when someone will benefit from more than others at certain times – but all are valid reasons.

▮▮ Pause
(15 mins):
Tell the groups how those who follow Jesus should also grow in their understanding and relationship/friendship with God. Tell them you are going to mention three key things that someone needs to do if they want to grow in their friendship with God and ask them to work out which each one is. Do this by showing a picture of each (see pages 107 and 108). (You could also give out the following verses to help them solve it.) Get their suggestions and then expand on each of them.

1   Reading the Bible (show picture of Bible)
Read Psalm 119:105
Bring out the importance of reading the Bible. If possible, have some relevant Bible reading notes to give out (see p? for details).

2   Going to church (show picture of people)
Read Acts 11:26, Romans 16:23 and Acts 15:4.
Recap on the importance of going to church.

3   Praying to God (show picture of hands praying)
Read Matthew 6:9
Talk about how we should pray regularly.

Fast forward
(10 mins):
Body or building game
In groups give out the names of the following objects they have to make by forming their bodies into the shape of the object. Give out points for the most realistic objects. Tell the groups they are all things you may find in the church building: chair/ font (you may need to show a picture so that they know what a font is)/ lectern, bible/ door.
Make up some of your own.

Tell the group that these are things we may find in the building. Yet the church is also made up of people. The church is not a building but the people. People who follow Jesus make up the church. Sometimes we make the mistake of thinking of the church simply as the building we go to on Sunday. Because the church is the people then the church is anywhere people who follow Jesus are.

Why have a building? Not all churches have a special building – some meet in a house. We meet together in a house or building to spend time with other Christians, to learn more about God and how best to follow Jesus today.

Peer pressure

Aim:

To explore ways in which Christians can face peer pressure.

Bible base: Genesis 37:12–36

You will need: two paper clock hands, *Joseph* video (optional)

Tuning in
(10 mins):
Who pulls the strings?

On the board draw a large clock face, with the hours numbered 1–12, and cut out two pieces of paper that can be used as the large and small hand of the clock. (This could be done equally well on an OHP.) Explain that you are going to be telling the time based on decisions that you make. Alongside the clock put up a key numbered 1–12 where each number represents someone who or something which might influence a decision that you make. Try to compile your list from suggestions from your group, eg mother, father, friends, boy/girlfriend, teachers, God, brothers and sisters, adult friend, youth leaders, TV, magazines…

Divide your group into two teams. Explain that you will give each team a decision that they must make and one person from that team will set the clock as follows: the big hand points to the biggest influence on that decision and the little hand will point to the second biggest influence. For example, take the question, 'Who influences where you go on holiday?' The biggest influence may be parents and the second biggest a magazine (holiday brochure). If parents are listed

in the key as number 3 and magazines as number 7, the person will set the clock at 7.15. While the person setting the clock (the player) waits outside, give the rest of the team the question and get them to write down the time that they think the player will put on the clock. Invite the player back in, give them the situation and ask them to set the clock. If both hands match, the team scores 10 points; if only one hand matches they score 5 points. The second team then plays its round and so on, with a new player from each team at the clock each time.

Situations could include (feel free to add your own): Choice of boy/girlfriend; where you go on holiday; your bedtime on a weekday; what GCSEs to do; which CD to buy; whether to go to church; what new clothes to buy.

Pause
(15 mins):
Input

There are a whole load of people and things that influence our decisions. Some of these are obviously trying to influence us for our own good (normally!) such as parents, teachers, God, friends, etc but some have less pure motives (such as TV advertisers). We need to be aware of what things/people are influencing us and then decide whether we go along with them or stand up against them.

Give a brief background account to the story of Joseph and his brothers in Genesis 37. Joseph was the favourite of the twelve sons of Jacob (who is also called Israel). The brothers were jealous of this favouritism and also resented Joseph's dreams that suggested that they, although older, would bow down and submit to him. In this story, Jacob has sent Joseph to check how his brothers are doing as they look after the sheep…
Read or act out the story of Genesis 37:12–36. You will need Jacob, Joseph, Reuben, Judah, a Midianite, Potiphar and a narrator, though extra brothers and Midianites would be useful. This could work very well, but if you don't feel up to it,

there is an excellent retelling of the story on Episode 1 of the SU video *Joseph*.

Play
(15 mins):
Brothers united

Look again at verses 19–21. Imagine how Reuben must have felt. What pressures were on him? What if he'd kept quiet? What did he risk by speaking out?

Reuben was under tremendous pressure. He was being egged on by his brothers to do what he knew was wrong. It would have been much easier for him to have kept quiet and gone along with them. But he knew that was wrong. So he was prepared to put himself at risk and stand up for what was right. Sometimes we can feel under great pressure to go with the crowd rather than stand up for what's right. It is important to ask God to give us the strength to do so.

In groups of four, spend a few minutes coming up with a short play showing how someone copes when they are put under pressure in a particular situation, without giving in. (Possibilities include: smoking, shoplifting, under-age drinking, bunking school, etc) Watch the plays being performed and comment on the different approaches used to beat the pressure.

Fast forward
(5 mins):

Close your session by asking the group if any of them have ever felt pressured into doing something that they knew to be wrong. Did they give in to it? How did they cope? Follow this with a time of prayer, asking God to help you overcome the pressures that come your way.

12 Friendship

Aim:

To explore the qualities that make up a sound Christian friendship.

Bible base: 1 Samuel 18:1–4; 20:1–42;
2 Samuel 1:26 (David and Jonathan).
You will need: *Blood and Honey* video
(CTVC, optional, see Appendix).

Tuning in
(10 mins):
You're the judge

Give each person a piece of A4 paper. Ask them to fold it into four sections, open it out again and write the numbers 0, 2, 4 and 6 in each of the four sections. They should then tear their paper so that each person has four separate score cards.

0 means there is no truth in the statement.
2 means there is a bit of truth in it.
4 means the statement is generally true.
6 means that it is true.

Read out the following statements. After each one ask each person to vote by holding up the numbered card which comes nearest to their viewpoint. Add the scores each time.

★ *Friends tend to be of the same age.*
★ *Friends must have at least one common interest.*
★ *Friends must spend a lot of time together.*
★ *It is easier to be friends with people of the opposite sex.*

★ *Christian friendships are deeper than other friendships.*

Spend a few moments reflecting on the scores and taking any comments that people wish to make.

Pause
(15 mins):
Act out

Explain the background to the story of David and Jonathan. Saul was king and had a son called Jonathan who ought to have succeeded him. David (of Goliath fame) also lived at the king's court and became best friends with Jonathan – read 1 Samuel 18:1–4. Saul, however, became jealous of David's popularity and tried to have him killed, forcing him to go into hiding where he was dependent upon Jonathan's friendship.

If you have access to the Dramatised Bible you could read/act out the story of 1 Samuel 20. Alternatively, read and act it out from a normal Bible, using different people to take the parts of narrator, David, Jonathan, Saul and the boy (non-speaking part). Tony Robinson also tells this story brilliantly on the video *Saul Goes Bonkers*, from the *Blood and Honey* series (CTVC). After you have done this, explain that Saul and Jonathan were soon killed while David went on to become king. As far as we know, David and Jonathan never met again, though David was clearly deeply moved by his friend's death – read 2 Samuel 1:26.

What were the factors that made David and Jonathan's friendship so special? In pairs, come up with five suggestions and then put these onto a board/OHP.

Play
(10 mins):
A good friend

Play a version of the game '*I went to Paris and bought a...*' using the words '*A good friend is someone who...*' For example, the first person might say 'A good friend is someone who listens.' The second person would then say 'A good friend is someone who listens...' and then they would add their own idea, eg '...and who spends time with you.' The third person would recap both of these and add their own idea, and so the game goes on. Each person has to add their own quality to the list, drawing from personal experience or from what they have learnt from the story of David and Jonathan. If you want, you can devise forfeits for people as they drop out and prizes for the winners.

Fast forward
(10 mins):
Prayer – or share

If appropriate, spend time as a group in prayer, thanking God for your friends and particularly for the qualities that they bring to a friendship. Pray also for non-Christian friends, that you will have the opportunity to share with them the friendship that God offers through Jesus. Remember the qualities that made David and Jonathan's friendship so special.

If, however, you don't feel that your group would go for the prayer option, write the name of everybody there on slips of paper and put the slips in a bag. Each person must draw out one slip and write down three good qualities that this person has. Each person then folds up their paper and places it back in the bag. One at a time, a member of the group then pulls out a piece of paper and reads it out. No one will know who has written the comments but people will certainly feel encouraged by them.

45

Parents

Aim:

To explore the responsibilities that face Christian children and parents.

Bible base: Exodus 20:12; Colossians 3:20–21.
You will need: a video episode of *The Simpsons.*

Tuning in
(5 mins):
Highs and lows

Show a short extract of a clip from *The Simpsons* where the children are interacting with the parents (almost any episode will do!). Then ask the group to imagine that Homer and Marge were their parents... What would be the good things about that, and the bad? Your group can chat about this in pairs and then feed their answers in to the larger group.

NB. Do be aware that you are likely to have a number of pupils who have experienced divorce and for whom the whole subject of parents may be difficult to discuss. Make sure that they are not put on the spot or compromised in any way and let them know that you are available if they want to chat more personally at a later time.

Play
(15 mins):
Top Fives

Divide your group into four and give each group copies of the following categories to complete. Based on their own personal experience, what are:

1   The top five things your parents give you grief about?
2   The top five best things about your parents?
3   The top five parental sayings?
4   The top five of your sayings?

Also get them to complete the following four statements in their groups:

★ *If my parents could change anything about me, it would be...*
★ *The thing my parents most like about me is...*
★ *If I could change one thing about my parents, it would be...*
★ *If I could change one thing about myself for my parents, it would be...*

Allow each group to share its answers while you draw attention to any similarities that they have listed.

Pause
(10 mins):
Input

The one thing that you can be sure of with parents is that we've all got them. We may no longer live with them; we may not even have ever known them; but, although we didn't choose them, God did give us all two. It is often easy to look at other people's parents and wish that we had theirs rather than our own but, for the most part, all teenagers tend to face the same sort of problems with their parents. (Mention the Top 5 Current Hassles, which are likely to include what they wear, what time they come home, how much school work they do, etc.) Tensions tend to arise because, naturally, as teenagers we want to be doing things before our parents feel that we are ready for them.

God is very concerned about families and the relationships within them. Ask two people to look up and read out Exodus 20:12 and Colossians 3:20. What two requirements are asked of children? Is this good news or bad? Did you know that in Jewish culture children actually became adults at the age of 13? Do these verses still apply to us legally or morally and what about a parent's responsibility to the child? Read Colossians 3:21. If parents don't fulfil their responsibilities, does this mean that the children are excused from theirs? Remember too that when you become an adult, parents will still take some responsibility for you – and you for them! As they become older and perhaps, in old age, less able to cope, the initial child/parent relationship can almost take on a complete role reversal.

 ## Fast forward
(15 mins):
Open theatre

(This activity will work particularly well with an imaginative group.) Set up a table with four chairs at the front of the room. The group have to imagine that this is a dinner table where Mum and daughter, Michelle, are arguing about what time she has to come back from Dave's party. Ask for two people to play these parts. As the conversation develops, you can stop the action and bring in the father and Michelle's older brother, Phil. If other group members so choose, they can shout 'Pause'. The action then stops, the person who called out takes the place of one of the characters and the action then restarts. (This

can be a very effective use of drama, particularly if you can start with two fairly confident actors.) If time allows – or if you prefer – you could use the following scenarios, or come up with your own:

★ *Phil wants to go on holiday with his friends rather than with the family.*
★ *The parents want the children to help out more around the house.*
★ *Mum has found a packet of cigarettes in Michelle's room. (Parents are very anti-smoking.)*

Draw out some of the ideas that the drama has thrown up which may include:

★ *Communication needs to be at the heart of the parent/child relationship.*
★ *Parents normally act out of loving concern rather than a desire to be negative (even though it doesn't always seem that way!).*
★ *Negotiation and compromise are healthy. Obstinacy and confrontation are not.*

Finish with a time of prayer, thanking God for parents and praying for wisdom when dealing with them.

If you have any extra time, or if you want to follow this through in a further session, it would be good to explore how the shape of families has changed since Biblical times. Today it is quite normal to live alone or to be a single parent with cousins, parents and grandparents miles away. Compare this to Abraham's situation (Genesis 11:31) or even Noah's (Genesis 7:13). What are the advantages and disadvantages of having an extended family at home or close by? What would God's ideal be?

Boys and girls

outline

14

Aim:

To explore a Christian attitude and response towards boy/girlfriend relationships.

Bible base: 2 Corinthians 6:14–16.

You will need: two packs of playing cards, a selection of Problem Pages (vetted for anything too indecent!), an item that's currently 'in', a mug/T-shirt from a recent event and a wedding ring (see *Fast forward*.)

Tuning in

(10 mins):
Pairing off

On the board, put up 25 square pieces of card, labelled 1–25, in a 5 x 5 grid. On the reverse of these 25 cards *Blu-tack* 12 pairs of playing cards (ie 2 x 3 of hearts, 2 x 10 of diamonds, etc) in a random order, taken from two decks. On the final card put the Ace of Clubs. Divide your group into two and let the first group choose two numbers. If they happen to make a pair, they keep the cards; if not, the cards are returned and the second group takes its turn. The game continues until all the pairs have gone and only the Ace of Clubs is left on the board. Award a small prize to the winning team or to both, if it's a tie.

Make the point that sometimes life can seem much like the game. It's a real rush to get paired off because you don't want to be the Ace of Clubs that gets left behind. But is this really what God intends?

Pause

(15 mins):
Input

If you want to know about baldness, spots and mildew, the Bible is great. Just take a look at Leviticus 13. Unfortunately, if you want to know about whether it is right to ask Katie Baxter out, then the Bible isn't quite so clear-cut. In fact, the Bible doesn't really have much to say on the whole subject of going out with people at all. While you might think that this is a fairly major oversight on God's part, the thing is that going out with people just wasn't part of Biblical culture. Marriages were arranged and people married much younger.

On the other hand, just because there are no references in your concordance to *snogging, dating* (not to be confused with *dates*, as in the fruit) nor even a guide to good *chat-up lines*, this doesn't mean that the Bible doesn't have any helpful principles to follow. In fact, there are plenty of these to consider. Either write out the following verses on an OHP or ask each pair to look up one of the references. Ask the pairs to decide what guidelines for relationships the following verses suggest:

★ *Genesis 2: 20–24; relationships are God given. They are a good thing.*

★ *1 Corinthians 7:32–35; being single is a really positive situation.*

★ *2 Corinthians 6:14–18; it isn't good for Christians to partner non-Christians.*

Play
(10 mins):
Problem Page

Give out a selection of Problem Page letters (without the replies) from teen magazines – one letter per person would be ideal. (Read these first so that you can remove any that you feel are not appropriate for the age of the group.) Ask the group to get into threes (ideally mixed sex) to study their problems. One person reads out their letter, the second person tries to answer as they feel Jesus would do and then the third can comment on the reply given. If time allows each one should have a go at each role. Finish this section by asking how easy it is to be sure what Jesus would say or do.

Fast forward
(10 mins):
Odd one out

Hold up (a picture of) something that's currently very popular, a mug or T-shirt from a particular place/event and a wedding ring. Ask which is the odd one out and why. You should get an interesting range of responses but our answer is... the wedding ring. Having a boy/girlfriend is not about trying to be like everyone else and have the latest in-thing. They are not possessions. Nor do you go out with someone for the 'been there, done that, got the T-shirt' experience. A wedding ring, however, is a symbol of love that goes on without end and is a sign of commitment. While not all relationships will end up in marriage, the picture of what a wedding ring stands for is a good one to have in mind before embarking on one. After all, if you really couldn't *stand* the thought of being married to someone, there's probably not much point in going out with them, is there?

Finish the session with a few minutes in silence, allowing everyone an opportunity to think through their response to what they have learnt today. Close with prayer and make yourself available for further conversations!

School

Aim:

To explore how school fits in with God's view of our lives.

Bible base: Colossians 3:23,24.

You will need: three large sheets of paper.

Tuning in
(5 mins):
Hit, miss or maybe

Organise the chairs into a circle and, as you read out the following things about school, ask the group to sit on the floor if they don't like the item (miss), to stay on the chair if they don't mind it (maybe) and to stand on their chair (or just stand up) if they like it (hit). Go through the list quickly at first so that people are having to move quickly and instinctively, then do it a second time allowing people slightly more time to reflect and to explain why they have made their choices.

Homework	Maths
Assemblies	PE
Break time	The uniform
Friends	Detentions
School trips	Dinners
Parents' evenings	English
This meeting	Teachers
Going home	

Play
(15 mins):
Hot, medium, cold

Around the room, put out three large sheets of paper. (Try scrounging leftovers from your art department.) Label each sheet with one of the titles, *Hot, Medium* and *Cold*. Explain that, in the last section, you set the agenda. Now it is their turn. Invite your group to write on each of the sheets the things that they enjoy (**hot**), don't mind (**medium**) and don't like (**cold**) at school. As well as writing the item, encourage them to put a few words of why they do/don't like it. (Make sure, however, that you don't allow personal comments about people to be put on the 'cold' sheet.) When everyone has had a chance to write, read the comments aloud and take any comments or questions that arise.

Make the point that school is not an option. It is something that we have no choice but to attend. For most people, it will bring out a mixture of emotions. During each day there are times when we would all choose to be elsewhere, but there are also likely to be times when we are quite happy with who we are with and/what we are doing.

Pause
(15 mins):
Input

When Jesus was on earth, he treated people as whole human beings, caring for their physical, social, intellectual and spiritual needs. He healed those who were sick, built the disciples into a group of friends, challenged the rabbis and forgave sins. For Jesus, of course, the spiritual need was of great importance but he recognised that the spiritual bits in people's lives didn't exist in isolation from the rest of them.

In some ways school tries to do the same. It provides for your physical needs (PE, school dinners, etc), your social needs (break time, PSE), your spiritual needs (this meeting, assemblies) and, of course, your intellectual needs (lessons). The difference however, is that the focus is heavily on the intellectual and so the spiritual can easily be marginalised.

★ *How should Christians behave at school? Read Colossians 3:23 and 24.*
★ *What does this mean in terms of school work? Homework? Friendships? Joining clubs?*

Fast forward
(10 mins):
Role play!

Divide the group into pairs. Ask them to act out one of the following conversations in one minute.

★ *A pupil asking a Christian teacher why he keeps mentioning God in assembly.*
★ *A Christian pupil persuading his parents to let him off homework to go to a church event.*
★ *A Christian pupil talking to his youth leader. The teenager feels useless after having failed all his GCSEs.*
★ *A Christian pupil who doesn't try at school because he wants to be a missionary, explaining this to a teacher.*

Try to draw out from these conversations that school is an important place where Christians should work hard – but not just at their school work. It is important to look after yourself physically as well as to build friendships and to serve God. This does not mean that Christians will necessarily always succeed in these things (we've no reportings yet of angels popping down to help students pass exams they hadn't revised for), but it does mean that they should try. On the other hand, if they do fail their exams, they are not failures in God's eyes for he places much more value on people's spiritual state than on their academic qualifications (see Matthew 6:26).

outline
16
The environment

Aim:

To help the group understand their God-given responsibility towards the environment.

Bible base: Genesis 1:1 – 2:2, especially 1:26–31.

You will need: large sheets of paper, photocopiable activity sheet (p102); *Blu-tack*

Tuning in
(10 mins):
The creation game

Take 18 pieces of paper (A5); on 7 of them write the numbers 1 – 7 (1 number on each); on the other 11 write the following words. The correct order is as below (see Genesis 1):

1　Day and night
2　Sky
3　Land and seas; plants and trees
4　Sun and moon; stars
5　Birds; fish
6　Animals; mankind
7　Nothing

Put the numbered cards in order down the side of the board and scatter the rest of the cards around the board randomly. One at a time, give each member of your group 10 seconds to put the other cards next to the number according to which day they think God created them. Depending on the time available, and the knowledge of your group, you can give clues, help them out, etc. until the game is completed. (To help, and as an incentive, you could give out a small prize each time someone gets one right.)

Pause
(10 mins):
Stewarding

Photocopy and distribute the Activity Sheet (p102) and ask your group to work through it in pairs. After a few minutes, go through it together, allowing the group to give their views. Make the point that God has charged mankind with the privilege and responsibility of caring for his world. It is not ours to do with as we choose but, in a sense, we are tenants, caring for the property on behalf of our landlord. Christians often use the phrase *good stewarding* to describe the way in which God wants them to care for the environment. This draws attention to the fact that Christians feel that they should care for the order and safety of the planet, much as a steward cares for the order and safety of people at football matches or pop concerts, etc.

Play
(15 mins):
Green Day

In the middle of the room put down a few sheets of large paper and some marker pens. Invite the group to brainstorm a list of things that they could do practically to care for the world, and to write these on the large sheets. Display them and comment as appropriate. Then challenge the group to look through the list and pick out any that they could either do or draw attention to at school.

Try to draw up an Action Plan of things that you will do either personally, or as a group, to reflect your concern for the environment. Ideas might include a poster display to promote recycling, a litter pick-up, petitioning companies who are exploiting the world's resources or even organising a Green Day, which might include all of the above and a whole lot more.

Fast forward
(10 mins):
Prayer tree

In the blank leaf on their photocopied sheet, invite each person to write a one-line prayer to reflect their concern for the environment. On the board draw a tree trunk with branches and then invite the group to cut out their prayer and then come out and *Blu-tack* their leaf on to the tree. Finish your session with a time of quiet as one or two people read out the prayers from the tree.

If you have time, you may also want to use a time of quiet to reflect on what man has done to what God has created. There may be video clips, pictures and articles from magazines, or lyrics to pop songs that will help you to do this effectively.

Injustice

Aim:

To explore a Christian attitude and response towards injustice.

Bible base: Acts 4:32–37

You will need: coloured pens, newspapers, scissors, sticky tape, resources from *Tear Fund/World Vision*, etc, (see *Play*).

Tuning in
(10 mins):
Hats off!

Explain that you are going to start today's session with a fashion parade. They will be divided into groups of four and will have just six minutes to design a hat out of newspaper which will then be modelled by one of the group on the catwalk. The only restriction is that they can only use the materials that you provide. To most of the groups give plenty of newspaper but very little or no sticky tape and to just one or two groups give plenty of sticky tape/scissors/coloured pens but very little newspaper.

Watch what unfolds – which could range from the brutal as groups steal from one another, through to complete harmony as the groups pool their resources and work together – without comment. Hold the fashion parade after the time is up (with a neutral judge) and award prizes as you see fit.

Pause
(15 mins):
Discussion

This section will depend heavily on how the previous exercise went. Try to get the groups to describe how they felt when they realised that they hadn't got any sticky tape. How did the group with all the sticky tape feel when they realised that they were in a position of power? Was trading done fairly or dishonestly? Did people cheat? What feelings did they have as the situation changed? If they had their time again, what would they do differently? Did they consider all joining together into one large group and sharing all the resources equally?

Read out Acts 4:32–37. What did the disciples do to help the poor? What might we be able to do?

Play
(15 mins):
Doing your bit

Agencies such as *Tear Fund*, *World Vision*, etc (addresses in the Appendix), provide some excellent free resources – or it may be that there is a local worker who can come and visit you, or lend you a video of their work. Is there some way that you can get involved, perhaps by raising some money or ensuring that you move towards using fairly traded products (products that don't exploit the workers in the developing countries that produce them, by paying them a fair wage)? Perhaps you could publicise these in school. Above all, however, make sure that you don't just talk about the possibilities. Actually get out there and *do* some of them!

Fast forward
(5 mins):
Gone fishing

There is a well-worn (and possibly overused) saying that if you can give a man a fish, you feed him for a day, but if you can give him a fishing rod, you feed him for a lifetime. What does this mean about what we give and how we give it? Do we still need to give fish (metaphorically speaking) to those who are underprivileged? Finish with a prayer, thanking God for the plenty that he has entrusted to us and asking him to guide us in using it wisely for the good of all people.

Addictions

outline **18**

Aim:

To explore a Christian attitude and response towards addiction, whether to alchohol, drugs, shoplifting, etc.

Bible base: 1 Corinthians 6:19,20.

You will need: a ball of wool, scissors, a guest speaker (optional – see *Fast forward*).

Tuning in

(10 mins):
Hooked

Ask for a volunteer to play an important role in a story that you are about to tell and place them at the front on a chair. As you tell the following story, you should wind a ball of wool round and round the person, fairly tightly. (Note that this is just an outline. Don't read it out word for word as it will work much more effectively if you embellish it with details of your own.)

Terry had always been one for a dare. If his mates said 'I bet you wouldn't dare...', he'd be certain to do it. Climb that tree? No problem. Juggle eggs? Easy. Put salt in the teacher's tea? Well, OK then. It was just fun, you know. Nothing illegal.

Then he'd fallen in with the wrong crowd and had started to shoplift. Nothing major. Just a few sweets... Then a packet of biscuits... Some cigarettes... And some more. In many ways he quite enjoyed it. He got quite a buzz as he stuffed the things in his pockets and nonchalantly walked out of the shop. It had even been quite a laugh

when old Mrs Shenley at the newsagents had spotted him and he'd had to leg it out at top speed. Anyway, it was just a game. A bit of harmless fun. After all, he could stop whenever he wanted. Couldn't he? (At this point ask your volunteer to try and break through the wool that has tied him to the chair. If you talked slowly and looped fairly quickly they will have no chance.) Ask the group if there was a point when Terry could have broken free of the habit.

Pause

(10 mins):
Input (1)

The story illustrates how easy it is to get tied up in a bad habit to such an extent that you can't break free of it. Of course, the person didn't realise how entangled they were until they tried to break free – and by that stage it was too late. That's how addictions work. People start on something as a bit of harmless fun, for a laugh or for kicks, but before long it can turn into a habit and so into an addiction that enslaves them.

There are two ways that Terry could break free. (Demonstrate these as you talk.) Firstly the wool could be unravelled and gradually he could work himself free. Alternatively, even when he is bound tightly by the wool, he could be freed immediately by the use of a sharp pair of scissors.

In John 8:36, Jesus says: '... If the Son sets you free, you will be free indeed.' In pairs, discuss what this verse might mean for Terry. In what ways might Jesus be able to set him free?

Play

(10 mins):
To what? To what?

Divide your group into threes and ask them to compile a list of five things that it is possible to become addicted to. (Explain that you don't want the names of five different drugs, but five different topics, eg drugs, alcohol, sex/pornography, shopping, eating.) Take the group's suggestions to compile a complete list on the board/OHP.

Ask each group to choose topics from this list and to consider ways that you might avoid getting addicted to them. Get them to think carefully about the reasons why a person may start to become addicted to something. Discuss your findings.

Pause

(5 mins):
Input (2)

People get addicted to these areas – and others – for a whole variety of reasons (refer here to some of the suggestions that were given above). Of course it is perfectly true that the addictions can be overcome through prayer and the power of Jesus. People who are addicted, however, are often also in need of professional (perhaps Christian) counselling and ought to be supported and encouraged to make use of this help.

Fast forward

(10 mins):
On the spot

There is nothing more powerful than hearing a first-hand account of how someone has come through an addiction by God's strength. If you know of anyone who has such a story, this would be a perfect opportunity for them to share their experience. Perhaps there may be a contact at one of your local churches who would be happy to do this. If you draw a blank on this, then spend the time praying for yourselves and those you know – that God will indeed set you free from those things which can so easily entrap you.

PS. Get hold of a copy of *Undrugged and Still Dancing: the facts on drugs and alcohol* by Debbie Goddard (SU, £4.99) for a readable, comprehensive look at the facts on drugs and alchohol.

Reading the media

outline
19

Aim:

To understand how the media can influence us and how Christians can respond to it.

Bible base: Romans 12:2; Philippians 4:8.

You will need: newspapers.

Tuning in

(5 mins):
True or false

Label one end of the room **true** and the other end **false**. As you read out the following statements, ask your group to move to the position that best describes their response.

- ★ *I watch more than two hours of TV on average each day.*
- ★ *Violence in horror films is so unrealistic that it doesn't affect you.*
- ★ *Problem pages in teen mags encourage you to do what you otherwise wouldn't.*
- ★ *I am more powerfully affected by what I read than by what I watch.*
- ★ *I am more affected by swearing/blasphemy than by sex/violence.*
- ★ *The media simply reflect what is going on – they don't promote it.*

At the end of each sentence, encourage one or two people to comment on why they have chosen to stand in their particular places. (Do not get into a discussion here however – simply accept the comments and move on.)

Play

(15 mins):
Sixty - second debates

Return to your original places and go through the statements again. Pause after each one and allow sixty seconds for any comments to be made before moving on to the next statement.

Encourage people to speak briefly and to the point. Try to include a diversity of opinions.

On The Board

Give out a copy of a newspaper(s) (your library might have some spare copies) and ask each person to choose a story from the news pages (not the sports section). Ask them to quickly read through it and then call out the main theme of the story (murder, sex, intrigue, etc). Write these on the board.

Pause

(15 mins):
Input

One of the media's biggest defences is that what they show doesn't actually influence people. To some extent this is obviously true. We don't watch Tom and Jerry and go out and attack our pets! On the other hand, major corporations pay executives thousands of pounds and invest vast millions to produce commercials which they know will influence those who watch them. Are TV stations suggesting that we are influenced by adverts but not by the programmes in between?

Also, most TV companies, when challenged about what they show on their screens – or newspapers/magazines, when challenged about what they print (such as the items you've just listed) – simply say that they are reflecting what is actually going on in society. This is true. Somewhere in the world each day people are having affairs, abusing children and committing atrocities of almost unimaginable evil. This does not mean, however, that these things are all that is going on. Nor does it mean that these things are in any way normal or acceptable. The problem is that when these are the only things we are exposed to, we can start to think that they are normal and acceptable.

★ *Ask someone to read out Romans 12:2 and Philippians 4:8. (If you were able to have these written out on an OHP or on the board beforehand, this would be helpful.)*

★ *In pairs, discuss what this might mean regarding a Christian's reading/viewing habits.*

Fast forward
(10 mins):
We say!

Divide into four groups and give each group one of the following scenarios:

Family 1: Don't have a TV or get newspapers because they don't want to be corrupted.

Family 2: Have no limits on what they read or watch. Freedom of choice is all-important.

Family 3: Are selective in their reading/viewing habits.

Family 4: Both parents are Christians and work in the media. The father is a news journalist on a national newspaper while the mother is a researcher on an Oprah-style chat show.

Ask each group to appoint a spokesperson who will try to defend the views of their particular family. Give them a few minutes to discuss their ideas but just *one minute* to explain their thinking. Conclude your session by reminding everyone that what we choose to read and watch does influence us to a certain degree. This can be a good thing – there are excellent programmes, films, articles, books, etc that can be entertaining, challenging, informative and helpful. But it is important not to swallow wholesale the warped view of the world that the media can portray at times. Moreover, God also calls Christians to work in the media where they can be salt and light for him and to enable them to present a more balanced world view.

Self-worth

Aim:

To understand how highly God values each individual.

Bible base: Genesis 1:27; Psalm 139:13–16; Matthew 6:26, 10:29–31; 1 John 3:16 (all on activity sheet, p?).

You will need: objects for *The Price Is Right* (see suggestions below), photocopiable activity sheet, pencils.

 ## Tuning in
(10 mins):
The Price Is Right

Play a version of the TV game show *The Price Is Right* where contestants are invited to guess the price of a variety of objects. Choose three contestants and have three items on hand for them to price (eg a pencil, diskman, pair of rugby boots, item of jewellery, watch, calculator). Bring these out one at a time and encourage the rest of the group to get involved by calling out 'Higher' or 'Lower', etc. Give a small prize to the person who is closest each time.

 ## Pause
(15 mins):
Input

We all agree that objects are worth different amounts, but what about people? Who is more precious: a tramp, Leonardo Di Caprio or yourself? (You could put up pictures to illustrate these if you want to.) What would your parents' answer be? What about the tramp's wife (or husband!)? What would God say? In one sense we are all worth the same – about £10. How? Well, each human body contains:

Fat – 7 bars worth; **Iron** – 1 nail's worth; **Magnesium** – for one dose of salts; **Water** – 6 buckets' worth; **Sulphur** – enough to rid 1 dog of fleas; **Phosphorous** – enough to tip 2200 matches; **Sugar** – enough for 7 cups of tea.

Total cost = approx. £10.

(Source: *Line Up For Assembly* by Joanna Pitkin, SU.)

So there's the good news. You are worth exactly the same amount as Madonna, Ronaldo or the President of the USA. And the bad news, that's worth less than the *Barry Manilow Greatest Hits* CD.

Give out the activity sheet (p103) and ask each person to work through the score card at the top of the sheet on their own and then to discuss their answers with a friend. As a group then read aloud the Bible passages included. Ask them to answer the three questions at the bottom of the sheet individually, and finally, as a group, discuss where their true value lies.

Play
(10 mins):
Positive and negative

Give each person four small slips of paper. On two of them ask people to write a few words or draw a picture that reminds them of particular situations where they were made to feel useless or where hurtful comments were said to them. (It is important to emphasise that these negative things will remain confidential unless people wish to share them.) On the other two slips ask people to write down positive comments that either people have said to them or that they would like people to say to them.

In the middle of the room place a waste bin and a hat/plate. Remind everyone that in God's eyes each one of us is unique, special, valuable and therefore the hurtful, negative comments that people make need not affect our self-worth. As a sign of this, ask the group to rip up those two slips of paper and throw them into the bin. God wants us to have a positive image of ourselves so ask the group to fold up their other two bits of paper and place them in the hat/plate. When everyone has done this, ask the group to collect two pieces from the bowl and then go round the circle reading these aloud.

Fast forward
(10 mins):
Special

Working in pairs, ask the group to write an acrostic (a poem or list where the first letter of each line forms a word or words), describing their worth in God's eyes, entitled:

<u>We are</u>
S
P
E
C
I
A
L

Read these out to conclude your session.

PS. You might like to get hold of a copy of *Who do you think you are?* by Steve Mawston, SU, £4.99. It looks at how young people can have a healthy self-image in the midst of the strong images presented by the media and the expectations of others.

Guidance

Aim:

To explore how God speaks to us all differently and how we need to seek him for direction in our lives.

Bible base: Mark 1:16–20, Psalm 23:3,4, 119:105; John 10:4, 16:13; Mark 1:35; Matthew 7:7,8; Romans 7:1–6.

Tuning in

(5 mins):

Spend some time worshipping God. Bring out God's interest in our lives. You may find the *Guidance passages* printed on the next page helpful....

Play

(15 mins):

We are all different. Show people the tree on page ? and ask which person on the tree they most identify with. Give a short amount of time to discuss who the people on the tree are. Bring out how we all have different personalities and each of us has a different understanding and experience of God. So how does God talk to us? What about different cultures where people do things very differently? We worship the same God but does he communicate with each of us differently?

Pause

(20 mins):

Read Mark 1:16–20. Tell the group that they are going to look at where discipleship started – the time when Jesus called the first disciples. Go on to briefly bring out the points below about following Jesus and walking with him.

★ *We must trust and obey God as the first disciples did.*
★ *It is not always easy to give everything up for Jesus.*
★ *Our lives need to be surrendered to him.*
★ *He has the best in store for us.*

Use this passage as a lead into the next part of the session.

How does God speak to us?

Spread several sheets of A5 paper around the room. Tell the group you want them to go around and write one way in which God speaks to people at the top of each page. It does not have to be a personal experience but simply a way in which God might speak to someone. Do this till all the sheets of paper have one way in which God speaks to us at the top of them. Then ask the group to go round them again and tick underneath the heading if it is a way in which God has spoken to them. If a title at the top of the paper has been repeated tick it only once. (You just need to put them together when adding the ticks up.) Spend time looking at how God speaks to us. Give an opportunity for people to share experiences.

Guidance passages:

Give out the following passages, at least one to each person. Spend time discussing what the passage has to say about God guiding us.

'Your word is a lamp to my feet and a light for my path.' (Psalm 119:105)

'He guides me in paths of righteousness for his name's sake. Even though I walk through the valley of the shadow of death, I will fear no evil, for you are with me; your rod and your staff, they comfort me.' (Psalm 23:3,4)

'When he has brought out all his own, he goes on ahead of them, and his sheep follow him because they know his voice.' (John 10:4)

'But when he, the Spirit of truth, comes, he will guide you into all truth. He will not speak on his own; he will speak only what he hears, and he will tell you what is yet to come.' (John 16:13)

'Very early in the morning, while it was still dark, Jesus got up, left the house and went off to a solitary place, where he prayed.' (Mark 1:35)

'Ask and it will be given to you; seek and you will find; knock and the door will be opened to you. For everyone who asks receives; he who seeks finds; and to him who knocks, the door will be opened. Which of you, if his son asks for bread, will give him a stone? Or if he asks for a fish, will give him a snake? If you, then, though you are evil, know how to give good gifts to your children, how much more will your Father in heaven give good gifts to those who ask him!'
(Matthew 7:7–11)

Spend a bit of time on Matthew 7:7 and 8. 'Ask and it will be given ...' Bring out how this passage is often misquoted to justify our asking for what we want. These verses are set in the context of Jesus talking about worry – how we shouldn't waste time worrying but trust everything to God who has our best interests at heart. If we're seeking God's will we should not worry, for we are in his hands and he will sort out everything as he's planned and for our good.

Bible test:

Point out that when we are looking at how God guides us, we should ultimately see what the Bible says. If the guidance that we think we are receiving contradicts the Bible then it is not from God. God has specifically given the Bible to help and guide us (Psalm 119:105) so it is important that we spend time reading it.

Wedding parallel:

Finish this section by reading Romans 7:1–6. Briefly talk about how the better the husband or wife knows their partner, the more they know what their partner wants them to do. Even when the partner is not there, they still have a pretty good idea what their partner would think about things they do. God describes our relationship as being like a marriage. The more we spend time with him, the easier it is to know what he would want us to do.

 **Fast forward**
(5 mins):
Finish by spending time praying that God would guide and direct us.

Discipleship (serving God)

outline 22

Aim:

To explore what it means to be a disciple.

Bible base: Luke 5:1–11; 2 Timothy 2:3,4; Matthew 6:33, 7:21,22, 19:21–23, 20:26; John 14:12; 1 John 4:7,8; 1 Corinthians 9:24,25; Revelation 3:5.

Tuning in
(5 mins):
Start with a short time of worship. You could choose a psalm of praise and read it aloud together.

Play
(10 mins):
Mention that we are going to be looking at discipleship (serving God). (The next activity requires small groups. You may want to split the group into smaller groups or stay together if you only have a few people.)

Mr/Mrs Disciple

Each group should have a large sheet of paper on which to draw a picture of Mr/Mrs Disciple. Around the picture write down as many qualities you can think of for the perfect disciple (what they should be like). Ask the group to put down any relevant Bible passage they know that backs up what they have written.

Pause
(25 mins):
Read Luke 5:1–11 (Jesus calling the first disciples). In the passage we see the first steps of the disciples recognising and following Jesus...

★ *Command* *To let down the nets*
★ *Obedience* *They did as Jesus asked. They obeyed.*
★ *Recognition* *Peter was convicted of sin (he fell on his knees).*
★ *Follow* *They left everything and followed Jesus.*

1 Why do you think that Jesus asked them to cast the nets in again? (Was he saying anything about himself?)
2 How did Peter discover he was a sinful man even though Jesus had not yet mentioned anything about sin?
3 What did they know about Jesus at this stage?
4 What would they be leaving behind to follow Jesus?

End the discussion by bringing out that if the disciples had said, 'No, we're too busy' or 'We don't want to follow you,' they would have missed out on the most exciting adventure of their lives.

What is a disciple?

Give out the following passages, at least one per person. In turn read them and discuss what they have to say about following Jesus.

'Endure hardship with us like a good soldier of Christ Jesus. No-one serving as a soldier gets involved in civilian affairs – he wants to please his commanding officer.' (2 Timothy 2:3,4)

'... Whoever wants to become great among you must be your servant.' (Matthew 20:26)

'I tell you the truth, anyone who has faith in me will do what I have been doing. He will do even greater things than these, because I am going to the Father.' (John 14:12)

'Dear friends, let us love one another, for love comes from God. Everyone who loves has been born of God and knows God. Whoever does not love does not know God, because God is love.' (1 John 4:7,8)

'Do you not know that in a race all the runners run, but only one gets the prize? Run in such a way as to get the prize. Everyone who competes in the games goes into strict training. They do it to get a crown that will not last; but we do it to get a crown that will last for ever.' (1 Cor 9:24,25)

'But seek first his kingdom and his righteousness, and all these things will be given to you as well.' (Matthew 6:33)

Half-hearted

Select some of the following passages and briefly comment on why following Jesus requires everything. It is no good being half-hearted. (Matthew 7:21,22; Matthew 19:21–23; Revelation 3:5)

Cost and reward

Split the group into two. Have one group list the costs involved in following Jesus (what makes it difficult, etc), while the other lists the rewards and benefits of following Jesus. Spend time bringing out how it is not always easy but that Jesus recognises this and helps us. There is, of course, also an eternal reward for us in heaven (see Romans 6:22,23).

Born again

Finish by bringing out how the Bible only mentions the term 'born again' (ie becoming a Christian) a couple of times, but that the concept of following/being a follower (or a disciple) comes across numerous times. Ask the group to go away and think through the difference there may be between the two. You could end by debating the somewhat provocative statement: 'The church is full of born-again Christians but not followers.'

▶▶ Fast forward
(5 mins):
End with a time of prayer, asking God to help us follow him effectively today.

Gifts

Aim:

To discover together what God has to say about gifts.

Bible base: 1 Corinthians 12:1–11; Romans 12:6–8; Ephesians 4:11–13.

Tuning in

(10 mins):

Spend some time in worship. Try to have given out different things for people to do prior to this meeting, eg reading a Bible passage, sharing what God is doing in their lives, a prayer or a short meditation. Encourage those people who don't normally take an active role to take part, but be sensitive to what they are realistically able or would want to do.

Pause

(30 mins):

Tell the group we are going to look at some of the gifts God gives us, using the SU method/approach to reading the Bible. You will find this method at the front of the SU reading notes. Mention Bible reading notes at the end as an encouragement to read the Bible daily. (See the Appendix for how to get free samples of Bible reading notes for your group.)

The five steps to help you read your Bible effectively are:

1 Pray
2 Read
3 Think
4 Pray
5 Share

Pray: Start off by asking God to help you understand and learn from what you are about to read.

Read: Read 1 Corinthians 12:1–11 You may wish to read the passage in a circle, with each person reading one verse at a time. You may also wish to read it twice, from two different versions of the Bible.

Think: Ask the group to think through the following on their own:

What have I read about God the Father, the Lord Jesus or the Holy Spirit in this passage? In these verses is there:

★ *A command to obey?*
★ *A promise to believe?*
★ *A good example to follow?*
★ *An example of a wrong thing to avoid?*

After everyone has had the chance to think through their response to the passage, give them an opportunity to share what they have discovered.

You may wish to look at the following passages and questions to enhance your study on gifts. Read 1 Corinthians 12:27–31, Romans 12:6,7 and Ephesians 4:11–13.

★ *List as many different gifts as you can think of.*
★ *Are some gifts more important than others? How important is speaking in tongues? Is this a gift for everyone?*
★ *Why has God given us different gifts?*
★ *Does everyone have the gift of healing? Why are some people not healed?*
★ *How can we know which gifts are appropriate for us?*

Pray: Spend some time asking God to help you to remember and put into practice the things he has been teaching you.

Share: Finish by telling the group to share something they have discovered or learnt from the study with others (not in the group) who would appreciate it.

Fast forward
(5 mins):
Spend time thinking about what gifts God has given you. You may wish to affirm a gift you recognise in someone else. Conclude this by thanking God for the gift he has given you and thinking through how you will use it for others. This could be done as part of a worship time.

24 outline

Witnessing/evangelism

Aim:

To look at our responsibility to tell others about Jesus.

Bible base: Matthew 28:16–20, Acts 1:8.

Tuning in
(5 mins):
Spend a short time praising God, giving thanks for what he has done for us, eg giving us the privilege of being his children.

Play
(15 mins):
Ask what comes into people's minds when you say 'Evangelism'. Use this as a means to introduce the subject.

To help explore our thoughts on witnessing/ evangelism do the sliding scale exercise. This is good to get people's thoughts focused before looking at what the Bible has to say.

Sliding scale

The sliding scale works by making a space up the middle of the room. At one end is the statement STRONGLY AGREE and at the other STRONGLY DISAGREE. You then make a statement and people have to stand in a place that reflects how strongly they feel about the issue. This is a gentle way of finding out where people stand on the matter as well as sensitively challenging them to discussion on their views. It is also good as a means of asking one side what they may advise

the other. (For example, with the statement, 'It is easy to talk to people about Jesus', you may ask the group who stand nearer the 'strongly agree' end to explain why they find it easy and then encourage them to share any helpful tips. Do the same with those at the 'strongly disagree' end too.

★ *Everyone who follows Jesus has a responsibility to tell others about Jesus. (If everyone says it's not their responsibility you may want to go straight to the Pause section and come back to the rest of the questions later.)*
★ *It is easy to tell people you are a Christian.*
★ *It is easy to talk to people about Jesus.*
★ *Jesus helps us to witness to others.*
★ *Our lives should be a witness to God. (How easy is this?)*
★ *We should be telling people daily if not hourly that they have to follow Jesus.*
★ *There comes a time when we should tell people directly and not avoid it.*

Pause
(15 mins):
Methods of evangelism:
Briefly list different ways in which the church reaches out to people and evangelises (shares the good news about Jesus Christ).

Read Matthew 28:16–20, 'The great commission'. Before discussing the following questions, briefly bring out the following: Jesus has died and come back to life. He encourages his disciples to tell others about him yet, from verse 17, we read some still doubted him (even though he was standing right in front of them). There will always be those who do not believe and who are blinded to the truth. Yet Jesus goes on to say that all authority is his, and therefore we can go and tell others. He is with us, helping us every step of the way – we are not alone.

1 What authority is Jesus talking about?
2 What difference does it make?
3 'Therefore go …' (verse 19) What is Jesus saying about our responsibility to tell others?
4 'Teaching them …' (verse 20) What responsibility do we have to nurture young Christians? (Bring out that we are not into 'hit and run' evangelism, but we need to think seriously about how we help someone who has just become a Christian to grow in their faith.)
5 'I am with you always.' (verse 20) In what ways is Jesus with us? What comfort can we draw from this?

Let's get practical

Start by reading Acts 1:8. When God gave the Holy Spirit, Jesus asked the disciples to be witnesses in Jerusalem, Judea, Samaria and to the ends of the earth. Note how they were to start where they were (in Jerusalem), then move further out to Judea then further out again to Samaria then ultimately into the whole world. The important thing is that they started where they were, in Jerusalem, just as we should start where we are now, ie with the friends we have, in the places we go.

Spend some time discussing both as a group and as individuals how you could take up the responsibility to tell people about Jesus. A simple suggestion would be to organise a meal to invite friends to. Remember that concentrating on a longer-term programme of relationship building is often far more effective than seeking to tell people the gospel when they're not ready to hear

it. You might like to plan some purely relationship-building, fun events with limited Christian content. Many who come to these events many not be interested in finding out about Jesus, but they may well be interested in getting to know some new people and enlarging their circle of friends.

Fast forward

(10 mins):
Finish by praying in the following order:
1 For people we know in the school/college (mention them by name).
2 Our country. For our leaders, etc and that as a nation we will turn back to Jesus.
3 The world. That the light of Jesus would shine throughout the world. You might want to pray for specific countries that are in the news at the moment.

Life – what's  the point?

outline
25

Aim:
To look at how life without God has no meaning and to show how God knows and loves us and brings meaning to life.
Bible base: Ecclesiastes 1:2,10,11, 2:1–3, 5:10; Psalm 139; Matthew 10:29,30.

Tuning in
(5 mins):
Start off by spending some time in prayer. We are looking at life so pray that God would use our lives to serve him in our schools and colleges, etc.

Pause
(30 mins):
Start off by asking if any one has ever spent time thinking how big the universe is.

Solar system
Can any of the group place the stars in the solar system in order? As a fun way of doing this you may wish to make ten cards with the names of the following on them: Sun, Mercury, Venus, Earth, Mars, Jupiter, Saturn, Uranus, Neptune, Pluto (these are in order of distance from the sun). They have to work out the correct order of the planets in terms of distance from the sun. You may wish to do this in smaller groups.

Using some of the following facts, bring out how vast the universe is:

★ *There are thousands of galaxies, each of which contains huge numbers of stars.*
★ *Our galaxy (the Milky Way) contains about 100 billion stars.*
★ *The Milky Way is 100,000 light years across from one end to the other.*
★ *The sun is 30,000 light years from the centre of the Milky Way.*

Ask if anyone else has any other facts. Because we live in a huge galaxy, how can we be convinced God is interested in our lives?

Pursuit of meaning
Since the beginning of time, people have been in pursuit of the meaning of life, trying to discover what their life is all about. The fact is, if you take God out of the equation, then we struggle to find any meaning. This is what the book of Ecclesiastes is all about. You may want to quote a few relevant verses for response. Here are some you may wish to try:
Ecclesiastes 1:2,10,11 (Everything is meaningless, nothing is new.)
Ecclesiastes 2:1–3 (Pleasure is meaningless.)
Ecclesiastes 5:10 (Riches are meaningless.)

Quotes:

Give out the following quotes so each person has at least one. Spend some time reading them out and commenting on them. They are quotes from famous people trying to make sense of life:

Life is like a broken pencil. Pointless.
Edmund Blackadder

I never had the answer to anybody's life. I don't have the answer to my own.
Bruce Springsteen

The man who regards his own life and that of his fellow creatures as meaningless is not merely unfortunate but almost disqualified from life.
Albert Einstein

God does not play dice.
Albert Einstein

God not only plays dice. Sometimes he throws them where they cannot be seen.
Stephen Hawking

Man – a being in search of meaning.
Plato

Space is big, really big. You just won't believe how vastly, mind-boggling big it is.
Douglas Adams

Everything's got meaning, if you can find it.
Lewis Carroll

I truly believe that something or someone or some force put me here for a reason.
Madonna

Life is a lemon (and I want my money back).
Meatloaf

We come. We go. And in between we try to understand.
Rod Steiger

I am the way the truth and the life.
Jesus

I have come that you might have life and have it to the full.
Jesus

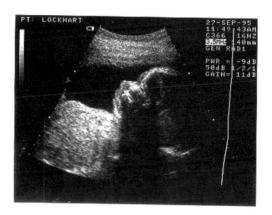

Read Psalm 139 and discuss the following:

1 If God knows all about us how much time do we spend getting to know him?
2 According to this passage, what value do we have in God's eyes?
3 Does God really know all about us? How does that make you feel?
4 How can God know all our evil thoughts and still love us?
5 It can be easy to see ourselves as special in God's eyes but what about those we don't like? Are they equally special to him?

Fast forward
(10 mins):
Start by showing the scan of a baby and use this as a lead into a time of worship. Bring out how God made each one of us and he created us in his image. 'I'm me and I'm good cos God don't make junk,' as a young black American so eloquently put it. We are special in his eyes. He gives us value. He also has a plan for our lives so let's praise him. You may also wish to quote Matthew 10:29,30 which says that God even knows how many hairs are on our heads!

Euthanasia

Aim:

To debate euthanasia and the Christian response to it.

Bible base: Ecclesiastes 3:1–8; John 11:34–44.

Tuning in
(5 mins):

Spend some time worshipping God, the giver of life. You could listen to some music on a CD/tape or sing, or you may prefer to pray your praise.

Play
(5 mins):
Game of life

Play the game of life by telling the group you are going to read out a list of activities we all do. They have to guess how much time the average Westerner spends in each of these activities during their life. You may want to give them a couple of options to guess the correct answer... How long does an average Western professional spend:

Waiting at red lights?	6 months
Opening junk mail?	8 months
Looking for things?	1 year
In wasteful meetings?	3 years
Being interrupted?	4 years
Waiting in queues?	5 years
Eating?	6 years
In the bathroom?	7 years

Pause
(30 mins):

Read Ecclesiastes 3:1–8 ...a time for everything ... 'a time to be born and a time to die... a time to weep and a time to laugh, a time to mourn and a time to dance ...' Ask the group what these verses have to say about life and death. Briefly discuss what they think God's response to death is. Read John 11 and use Lazarus as an example to show the pain Jesus felt when his friend died. God did not create mankind to die but it's one of the consequences of our action in sinning (Romans 5:12–14).

Ask the group to come up with a definition of what euthanasia is. The dictionary defines it as: 'The act of killing someone painlessly.' Go on to discuss the following two questions:
★ *If someone is going to die anyway, is it ever justifiable to speed up the process?*
★ *If someone is on a life support machine that they will never come off, is it ever justifiable to turn the machine off?*

(Note: When we look at euthanasia, we need to be sensitive with one another, especially as there are different views on the subject and people may well be in situations where it is a pressing issue.)
Read John 11:34–44. Discuss the following:
What was Jesus' reaction to death?
What do you think was going through Jesus' mind?
Some people die in situations that make no sense to us. What do you think God's reaction is?

Bring out how there are situations today that don't make sense to us – eg a young person's sudden death – yet we see the heart of Jesus in verse 35. Jesus wept – real tears.

There are two kinds of euthanasia. Tell the group that after you describe them there will be a chance to talk about both of them and to ask whether they should be allowed in our country:

Active euthanasia: As its name suggests, this involves actively taking steps to end someone's life by, for example, giving them a lethal injection. Active euthanasia is illegal in this country.

Passive euthanasia: This involves giving patients as much comfort as possible without taking positive steps to keep the person alive, eg not resuscitating someone after they have had a heart attack.

Debate active and passive euthanasia using the following questions for guidance:

1 Who do they think should give the lethal injection in active euthansia? How might the person feel about it?

2 Who makes the choice: the patient, the doctor or the relatives? (What happens if the patient is too ill to make the choice?)

3 Could Christians ever support passive euthanasia?

4 Is there a sense in which humans are playing God at any stage?

5 The twentieth century has seen such advances in medicine that people can now be kept alive who otherwise would certainly have died. In other words, medicine might be seen as stopping nature from taking its course. Is this a fair view?

Case study

Tell the group to imagine that they are a doctor. A patient called Terry comes to them who wants to end his life. Read out the following profile:

★ *Terry has lung cancer.*
★ *As a result his breath smells bad.*

★ *He is in a great deal of pain.*
★ *He finds it difficult to swallow and sometimes struggles to breathe.*
★ *He is depressed.*

Ask them to discuss Terry's situation. Would they support euthanasia in his case?

Take a vote. Afterwards explain that the scenario was actually based on a true situation of a patient in a hospice. The doctor did not allow Terry to die but instead dealt with each symptom:

★ *He gave medication to reduce swelling and clear up the smell.*
★ *He gave appropriate treatment to greatly reduce the pain.*
★ *He discovered that Terry was a great Middlesborough supporter but that he had not been able to get to a game for years. To deal with his depression, it was arranged for him to go to a game.*

Some time later the doctor asked Terry whether he still wished that they had ended his life. 'No' was the reply. 'I have lived more in these past few days than I have in the whole of my life. I am now going to die a happy man.'

Sometimes in facing death there is an opportunity to put things right and to sort things out.

Finish by asking what our response should be to the question of euthanasia. How should we, as Christians, help someone facing death? There is, of course, always the chance that the person may go on to make the greatest discovery of all before they die – Jesus.

Fast forward

(5 mins):

Say that this is a very difficult subject that you've only been able to look at very briefly today. End with a time of prayer and pray that the church will meet its responsibility to help people who are going through difficult times.

Why me? (personal suffering)

outline
27

Aim:

To move towards an understanding of why people suffer.

Bible base: Romans 5:12; Job 1:6–12; Psalm 103:8–14; Matthew 11:28–30; Revelation 7:13–17. You will need: recent newspaper cuttings to set the scene for the *Tuning in* section (optional) .

Tuning in
(15 min):
It can't be...

Consider the following scenarios (read them out or, better still, write on the board/OHP):

★ *An 18-year-old boy was given a new sports car by his father as a birthday present. While taking some of his friends out for a spin, he lost control of the car and shot on to the pavement. Two elderly ladies, out shopping, were pinned against a wall and later died from their injuries.*

★ *It was just a normal school day with parents dropping off their children at the gates before going on to their work or back home. Two hours later, a gunman had gone mad and the school at Dunblane had lost several of its pupils and a teacher.*

Imagine that one of the ladies or one of the children was your grandmother or your child. What feelings might you have experienced as you first heard the news of the incidents? List these on the board. What feelings might you have for those who were responsible? List these, too. Then, in pairs, produce a list of questions or comments that you might have said to God either in the immediate aftermath of the incident or over the following weeks as you had time to reflect on what had happened. Share these together.

Pause
(20 min):
But why?

When people are faced with tragedies such as the ones outlined above, they frequently ask the question 'Why me?'. In other words, why should such things happen to *them* rather than to anyone else? Is it part of God's personal retribution scheme for something that they have done wrong? Some people blame God for not preventing the incident while others might even go so far as to blame God for causing it. So what does the Bible have to say on the subject of suffering? Is it personal? Is it God's fault? Did he cause it?

In pairs again, imagine that you are a minister and one of the relatives from the stories above has come to question you about what has happened. What reasons might you offer? Spend 5 minutes discussing this.

The Bible doesn't give any easy answers to the question of suffering but it does point to some principles:

★ *Sin entered the world through Adam and, ever since, people are born to be naturally sinful. No one is perfect – some people just commit more heinous crimes than others – see Romans 5:12.*

★ *Free will. God has given mankind free will. This means that they can perform actions that have consequences. God certainly could intervene, but to do so would take away man's free will to choose what he does. And where would it end? Would we expect God to intervene just as we were about to cut ourselves shaving?*

★ *God does not cause suffering for the sake of it. In Job 1: 6–12 God allows Satan to torment Job (again showing where true power lies), but to inflict pain and suffering maliciously would be completely against his nature (see Psalm 103:8–14). It is true to say, however, that God has brought about pain and suffering in order to bring people back to himself (see Numbers 21:4–9), but this is always for a purpose (see Hebrews 12:6–11).*

★ *It's not personal. God has not picked you out for suffering because of something that you have done. He will, however, come to you personally to offer you love and support during times of difficulty (see Matthew 11:28–30).*

★ *It's not permanent. For those who trust in God, suffering will only be a temporary thing and part of this world. In heaven, there will be no pain or suffering (see Revelation 7: 13–17).*

Are any of these reasons hard to accept? Are there any others that you would add? If you were talking to someone who was going through great suffering, would you try to share all these reasons immediately? Which ones would you choose to emphasise first? Why? Do people need comfort for their heads or hearts first?

 ## Fast forward
(10 mins):
Prayer time

Ask if there are any in the group who are going through times of pain at the moment. Pray specifically for them and their situations. Pray too for others you know who are going through difficult times. These could be people known personally to you or people you know of through TV or newspaper stories. Ask that God will comfort them and meet with them personally in their time of mourning or suffering. Finally, finish by praising God that:

★ *He is able to bring good out of tragedy.*
★ *He is a God of love who longs to heal the broken-hearted.*
★ *He defeated the devil on the cross through Jesus and suffering and pain will one day be done away with.*

75

Why us? (natural disasters)

Aim:

To move towards an understanding of why there is suffering caused by natural disasters.
Bible base: Genesis 3:1–19; Romans 8:18–22.
You will need: Video footage or newspaper cuttings concerning recent natural disaster(s), a map or globe (optional).

Tuning in
(15 mins):
Disaster

Unfortunately, the chances are that whenever you choose to do this session, there will be coverage in the media of a natural disaster somewhere in the world. (This may be drought, flooding, avalanches, volcanoes, hurricanes, tornadoes or lightning.) It would be good if you were able to show some news footage on a video or some photos from newspapers/magazines to introduce the topic. If you really are struggling, however, you could opt to show a section from a video such as *Twister*.

Insurance companies tend to insure houses and property against what they refer to as 'Acts of God'. On a sheet of paper brainstorm the sorts of things that you think they are alluding to. Why do you think insurance companies use this description? Is it a fair one? What other names might they use?

People who have gone through such experiences often have many of the same concerns and questions as those suffering a

tragedy inflicted by another human. They may, however, feel an even greater anger towards God as they cannot blame any particular people and so place the responsibility firmly at their doorstep.

Although many of the reasons that you identified in the previous outline will be valid here too, there is often still an overriding belief that somehow God is responsible. So what else does the Bible say?

Pause
(20 mins):
Is it you, God?

The Bible starts in Genesis 1 with the account of God creating the world. The refrain throughout is 'and God saw that it was good'. Now, clearly, flooding and drought, etc are *not* good so what went wrong? Read Genesis 3:1–19. (It would be good if different people read the parts of the serpent, Adam, Eve and God.)

As a result of Adam and Eve's disobedience, what punishment is given to a) the serpent? b) Adam and Eve?

This section of the Bible is referred to as 'The Fall' as it describes how Adam and Eve fell away from God. But it is not just the people who fell from God's original design who are affected. Look carefully at verses 17 and 18. What else has gone wrong? At The Fall the whole of God's creation was spoiled. The whole natural harmonious order of things was disturbed. Now look at Romans 8:18–22 (not an easy bit!).

★ *What is the link between the Genesis verses and verses 20 and 22?*

★ *What is the hope of verse 21?*

So, natural disasters occur as a result of The Fall and creation, like mankind, will have to go through suffering in this life until Christ comes again. But can all disasters be put down to The Fall? Are any of man's more recent actions responsible? In pairs discuss what else might be contributing to events, such as: deforestation, use of CFCs leading to the hole in the ozone, global warming, the melting of the polar regions, etc). Share these ideas as a whole group.

Mention here that some people actually choose to put themselves in dangerous situations, ie everyone knows that the San Andreas fault is live and that there will be a major earthquake along it at some point, but people still choose to live along it in cities such as San Francisco, even though they know they are at risk.

Fast forward
(10 mins):
Prayer time

Spend some time praying for those people/countries who are presently going through natural disasters. (It would be good if you could point out these places on a map/globe, if necessary.) Pray particularly for those who have lost friends and relatives and for those who are still in a time of suffering. Pray too for the aid agencies who are working there. Ask God to give them the energy to persevere and the wisdom to know how best to help.

See if there is a way that you can help practically. Is there a need for blankets, clothes, food or money? Are you able to raise/give money to those who are working in the disaster areas?

We need you (war)

Aim:

To explore a Christian attitude and response towards the question of war.

<u>Bible base: Revelation 12:7–9; Matthew 5:9, 38–46, 24:4–8; Luke 22:47–51; Psalm 44:1–8; Romans 13:1–2.</u>

Tuning in
(15 mins):
What war?

Read out the following quotes, pausing after each one to allow people the opportunity to respond to them:

War is good for absolutely nothing.
Edwin Starr

Advise none to marry or go to war.
George Herbert (1640)

In war, whichever side may call itself the victor, there are no winners, but all are losers.
Neville Chamberlain (British Prime Minister 1939)

War makes rattling good history.
Thomas Hardy (1840–1928)

There is many a boy here today who looks on war as all glory, but, boys, it is all hell.
General William Tecumseh (1880)

Go round your group, asking each person to call

out the name of a war that they have either read or heard about. Depending on the size of the group – and their knowledge of history – you might want to go round several times. Explain that you will be concentrating on two questions:

★ *Is war avoidable?*
★ *How should Christians respond to war?*

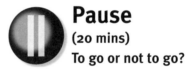

Pause
(20 mins)
To go or not to go?

Does anyone know where the first war broke out? Read Revelation 12:7–9. Even in heaven, where all ought to have been perfect, war broke out. (In this passage, the dragon stands for an angel, Lucifer, who became jealous of God and rose up against him.) Jesus also spoke of the outbreak of wars. Read Matthew 24:4–8. Much as we would long for peace, there has always been and always will be war. It is inevitable because it doesn't come naturally for human beings to live at peace with one another. That is not to say that wars are right, nor indeed is it to say that *all* wars are inevitable. But it does mean that we should not be surprised when we hear of wars breaking out.

When faced with the call of going to war, Christians have usually responded in one of three different ways:

Pacifist: A pacifist is someone who refuses to fight. People may be pacifists for a variety of reasons, but a Christian may look at verses such as Matthew 5:38–48 and Luke 22:47–51 and decide it would be wrong to fight. In pairs look up these verses and discuss whether they have a valid point.

Conscientious objector: A conscientious objector would not refuse to fight on principle in any situation but would look at each different situation on its own merits. Thus, if the person felt that the war was justifiable (perhaps to defend religious freedom or to overcome evil oppressors), then they would be prepared to fight. If they felt, however, that a war was not justified (perhaps motivated by a desire for power or out of greed), then they would not fight. Again, in pairs, discuss whether you feel this is a justifiable position to take.

Soldier: This person would be prepared to fight for their country, perhaps thinking of all the wars that God was involved in – see Psalm 44:1–8 – or because they want to be obedient to the call that their leaders make on them – see Romans 13:1,2. In pairs decide what other reasons Christians might give for being prepared to fight.

Of course, Christians have responded in other ways too: many volunteer to help in the medical corps and many soldiers – from a variety of faiths, or none – have paid tribute to the work of Army Chaplains.

If Christians have prayed through such

questions and come to different conclusions does this mean that some of these responses are necessarily wrong? Have some people clearly not obeyed God's answer or is it possible for three Christians to pray through the same issues and be led to different responses?

 Fast forward
(10 mins):
Prayer time

Read aloud Matthew 5:9. Spend time praying for those who serve in the Armed Forces and pray particularly for Christians and those working as Army Chaplains. Thank God for the time of relative peace in which we live. Pray for politicians and national leaders; that they would recognise that their authority comes from God and that their positions bring with them a responsibility to work towards peace.

We're after you (spiritual warfare)

Aim:

To explore what spiritual warfare is and how it affects Christians.

Bible base: Ephesians 6:10–18; 1 Peter 5:8; Matthew 4:1–11, 16:16–20, 18:18,19; Hebrews 2:14,15.

Tuning in
(10 mins):
Paired off

In Ephesians 6:10–18, Paul describes the armour of God with which all Christians should be fitted. But which piece of armour goes with which Christian quality? Before reading the passage, write the names of the pieces of armour on the board and then read out one of the qualities (taking them in a random order). Ask for a volunteer to write it up next to the piece of armour that they think it matches. Keep going until they have either solved it or given up.

belt	truth
breastplate	righteousness
boots	readiness of the gospel
shield	faith
helmet	salvation
sword	the word of God

Some pieces of armour are specifically designed for defence purposes – to keep you safe from attack. Other parts are offensive – to help you go on the attack. How many of the bits of this armour are for defence purposes? And for attack?

Pause
(20 mins):
Attack or defence?

Read through Ephesians 6:10–18.

- Who are we fighting against (v12)? Compare this with 1 Peter 5:8.
- What should we do (v13)?

In spiritual matters, it is important to grasp that the devil is the one who is either on the attack or looking out for ways to attack and the call to Christians is to defend themselves. Most of the armour, therefore, is designed with defence in mind. Three times Paul uses the word *stand* (as opposed to *advance* or *attack*, in the Ephesians passage). Note also how 1 Peter 5:9 uses the word *stand* in this context. In pairs, discuss why you think there is such an emphasis on defence. Is it being negative or realistic?

But spiritual warfare is not only about taking defensive measures. There is also a place for attack. What weapons might we use to go on the offensive (Ephesians 6:17,18)? To see one of these in action read through the whole account of Jesus' temptations in Matthew 4:1–11. Note how Jesus is actually able to quote the truth of scripture immediately to overcome the devil's lies.

★ *What scriptures do we know that we could use against the temptations that we face?*
★ *Do we know where to find them?*
★ *How could we improve our knowledge of the Bible?*

Now read Matthew 18:18,19 (compare to Matthew 16:16–20). These verses are talking about prayer:

★ *Why is prayer important?*
★ *Why are prayer meetings important?*
★ *What sort of things ought we to be praying about?*

Although there is clearly a spiritual battle going on, it is important to emphasise that Satan has already been ultimately defeated by Christ on the cross (see Hebrews 2:14,15). Of course, until Christ comes again, the devil can – and does – still fight against all things good. We are only too aware of that in our lives and in the world around us. But we must be in no doubt that his fate is sealed already and that Christ is assured of the victory.

Fast forward
(10 mins)
Prayer time

Start by thanking God for the victory that Christ won over evil through his death and resurrection. Thank him too for the armour that he has given you to protect you from the devil's attacks and for the gifts of his word and prayer that enable you to fight against the devil.

Pray for any you know who are struggling spiritually at present. Pray also for yourselves that you will be protected from attack and that, through God's Holy Spirit, you will be able to stand firm.

Either take a period of quiet to reflect individually on what you can do to increase your knowledge of the Bible and how you might pray more effectively or, as a group, discuss these things. Try to come to decisions that you can follow through ... and then follow them through!

(31) outline **Harvest**

Aim:

To look at things we should give thanks for, and at our responsibility to give to others.

Bible base: Matthew 6:1, 25:41–43.

You will need: a bar of chocolate, photocopiable activity sheet (see p.)

Tuning in

(10 mins):

Give each person a photocopy of the activity sheet (see p104). Tell the group it is a competition to see who can find the person that likes each of the things mentioned and to get their signatures. (Limit the number of times they can ask the same person, depending on how big the group is.)

Thanksgiving

Tell the group that they are going to think about Harvest. Churches often hold a Harvest service they call 'Harvest Thanksgiving'. We are going to look at Harvest by focusing on the word *Thanksgiving*.

Thanks brainstorm: Split into groups and give each group a large sheet of paper and pens. Ask them to write 'Things We Enjoy' in the middle and draw a circle round it. Around that, ask them to write down as many things as they can think of that they enjoy (ie something they eat, something they do).

Play

(15 mins):
Dear God

Photocopy the *Dear God* postcards and complete them by writing things on them that they want to thank God for. Stick the completed cards to a large poster at the front for all to see. (You could make the poster look like a brick wall to liven things up.) Spend time looking at the things they want to say thanks for. Read Psalm 107:8,9: 'Let them give thanks to the Lord for his unfailing love and his wonderful deeds for men, for he satisfies the thirsty and fills the hungry with good things.' Talk about how God give us all good things. He likes it when we enjoy them and are happy.

Say a prayer thanking God for the things they have written down.

Giving

Remind them of the things they love. Bring out a bar of chocolate and talk about how you love chocolate (the bar needs to be big enough for everyone to have a piece). Talk about how it was bought to give to the group. Start handing bits out. Give several pieces to the same person and decide to keep the rest yourself. Have fun with this until you end up with several in the group who don't have any. Talk about how unfair it is; there is enough to go around yet not everyone has a piece. Ask them why this is (particularly discussing your greed at keeping the most for yourself). Ask the group what the right thing to do would be. This, of course, would be to share out the chocolate equally. Do this, then go on to talk about how God has given the world enough food and resources but that the few keep the majority of the food to the cost of the many. Ask for a list of reasons of why people are so greedy.

There's a thought
(10 mins):
Brainstorm

In the same groups as before, brainstorm how God feels about our greed. Read Matthew 6:1. Talk about how we should give to those in need and how we should use the things God has given us to help others – without shouting or boasting about it. Read Matthew 25:41–43. Talk about how, when we do things for other people, it is as if we are doing them for Jesus. Read Matthew 25:40: 'I tell you the truth, whatever you did for one of the least of these brothers of mine, you did for me.'

Fast forward
(10 mins):
Giving

Briefly talk about how we should not only give of the money and possessions we have but also give of ourselves by doing things to help others. Read the following poem:

THE MAN WHO DID GO

I know a man who did go
He went to those forgotten by all
He went to those unnoticed by others
He went to those who needed help
He went to those who needed care
Those who had no earthly wealth
Those who felt of little value
Those in real need
A man willing to risk
Unpopularity from those around
The risk of getting too involved
The risk of infection

A man willing to give
Of his time
Of himself
Of what he had
A man they call Lord
LORD JESUS

© Bruce Lockhart

Finish by asking who around them might need their help. Who could they practically go to? Who could they give of themselves to?

Hallowe'en

outline
32

Aim:

To show that there are many things we fear and which keep us away from God, but that we need to keep our eyes on God who understands all we go through.

(This outline aims to be a fun look at Hallowe'en from a Christian point of view. Be careful not to go into the ghosts and spooky stories too much. We don't want to promote an unhealthy interest in this area as the Bible warns us against this.)

Tuning in

(15 mins):
Play hangman to spell out the word 'Hallowe'en'.

Feelings game

Ask for two volunteers. Choose a task, such as buying a pair of shoes, and tell the volunteers only what emotion the task has to be acted out in. The rest of the group has to watch and guess what the emotion is.

Have emotions relating to Hallowe'en, such as suspicion, surprise and fear. (Make up some more of your own but end on fear.)

Poster of Hallowe'en

Show the group a large sheet of paper with the word 'Hallowe'en' written at the top. Stick or draw any images connected with Hallowe'en, eg witches, on the sheet. Ask the group what emotions come into their minds when they think of Hallowe'en (refer back to the emotions in the previous game to get ideas going). Write them down on the sheet of paper for all to see. What other thoughts come into their minds when they think of Hallowe'en?

When you have exhausted their ideas, explain that Hallowe'en was originally a Celtic festival for the dead, celebrated on the last day of the Celtic year – October 31. It was believed that on this night, spirits of the dead roamed around and bonfires were lit to drive them away. Even after November 1 became the Christian holiday of All Saints Day (celebrating some of the heros of the Christian faith), many people still clung to the old pagan beliefs and customs that had grown up around Hallowe'en. Most Hallowe'en customs are survivals from the Celtic festival and folklore tradition around it.

Point out that when you look at it Hallowe'en is not a positive thing to celebrate at all. In fact Hallowe'en celebrates what is essentially evil and negative providing the chance to get scared, spooked and to make light of evil. It is something we ought to actively avoid and present a positive alternative to.

Play

(15 mins):
Warnings game:
Draw out some road signs from the Highway Code and spread them around the room. Tell the group that each sign warns the driver of a car about something, and ask them to choose a partner. Give each pair a piece of paper and see which pair can work out all the warnings first.

God warns us to stay away from things which might be harmful to us or which are evil. This includes Hallowe'en.

Use the following passages to talk about how

we should stay away from what is bad/evil:
'Let no-one be found among you who sacrifices his son or daughter in the fire, who practises divination or sorcery, interprets omens, engages in witchcraft, or casts spells, or who is a medium or spiritist or who consults the dead.' (Deuteronomy 18:10)
'But the way of the wicked is like deep darkness; they do not know what makes them stumble.' (Proverbs 4:19)
'It is when he walks by night that he stumbles, for he has no light.' (John 11:10)
The trouble is, we sometimes see things that we know we shouldn't do but we are attracted to them because they sound adventurous.

The lighthouse warning:

A boat was sailing in Oban (Scotland). The crew thought they knew the waters well: they had sailed the seas for several years. They were always game for an adventure and there was no greater adventure than seeing how close they could sail along the edge of the rocks. Even though the lighthouse beamed out a warning, they would sail closer and closer looking for a greater adventure than the time before. Unfortunately, one day they sailed too close and when they went to turn from the rocks, they found the current was too strong. It swept the boat and crew crashing against the jagged rocks, tearing the boat into small pieces. The crew had not taken the warning seriously and, sadly, paid the price.

Hallowe'en sounds like just a bit of fun but the Bible clearly warns us to stay away from anything associated with the occult.

Show the poster of Hallowe'en as you reiterate the passages and briefly conclude this section with how we need to be very careful.

Pause
(10 mins):
The things Hallowe'en celebrates can pull us away from God. They focus on what is evil, in contrast to God, whose character is good and pure and who is concerned for our health and well-being. Read John 8:12.

Blind man's fetch

Play Blind man's fetch by splitting the group into two teams. One team goes to one end of the room while the other stands opposite them on the other side of the room. In the middle of the room, place an item they need to collect, such as a pencil case. Each team needs to choose a volunteer who will be blindfolded. At a given signal both blindfolded victims have to try and pick up the pencil case while the group members at either end try to help their volunteer by calling out directions. (This gets more tricky if you put obstacles in the way.) Meanwhile the other groups can also shout out wrong instructions to put the person from the other team off.

Give each pair a time limit and, after everyone has had a turn, repeat the game, this time allowing a guide to walk beside the volunteers giving instructions and so making it easier to hear.

Ask the people who were blindfolded how they felt. Then parallel the game to the effect Hallowe'en can have. Bring out how there are many things that can confuse or distress us, and which make it more difficult to hear God. We need to make sure we are listening to God and not trying to find answers or direction through something else, ie horoscopes, Ouija boards, etc.

Fast forward
(5 mins):
Finish by briefly mentioning that there are real dangers associated with Hallowe'en. It is not all just made-up fun but a time when people get preoccupied with what is evil. Evil is whatever is out to keep us away from God. You may wish to mention a time when you have felt pulled away from God.

NB. Be careful throughout this outline not to scare anyone or to give them an unhealthy interest in Hallowe'en but be clear and direct as to the Christian response. You may want to hold a fun, positive event that is nothing to do with Hallowe'en on that night, and invite your friends to it.

outline

33

Remembrance

Aim:

To enable the group to appreciate the importance of remembering.

You will need: items for the *Can you remember?* game, newspapers (optional).

Tuning in
(15 mins):
Can you remember? game

Split the group into smaller groups and give each group a piece of paper and pen. Tell the groups that you are going to show a variety of objects. (Collect about 20 different items beforehand – they can be things normally found in a classroom or school bag.) After you have finished showing them, they have to write down as many as they can remember. See which group can remember the most.

Tell the group we are going to think about Remembrance Day – a time when we look back at the recent wars in this country and remember those who died for us, so that we can fully appreciate and enjoy the freedom we have today.

Newspaper models

Depending on your group, you may wish to do the following exercise: give each group a pile of newspapers and ask them to make models or to tear out the shapes of a tank, plane, submarine, etc. Award a small prize for the best one.

Poem

Read a poem or story highlighting the hardship and pain of war. (First World War poets such as Wilfred Owen are particularly effective – check out your library or English Department) After reading the poem, have a short time of open discussion about war and those who lost their lives while fighting. Does anyone know someone who fought in either of the last world wars?

Play
(15 mins):
Pray

Depending on your group, you may wish either to pray yourself or to ask if anyone else would like to pray.

Jesus' life

Life is the most precious thing we have. People have died so that we might have the life we have and live in peace. Jesus' life had a great effect, not just on our country but on the world past, present and future. Firstly, let's look at his life. Give each group a set of the following statements, each written on different pieces of paper. See if the group can place them in the correct chronological order.

★ *Jesus is born in Bethlehem*
★ *Jesus chooses people to follow him*
★ *Jesus turns water into wine*
★ *Jesus heals a sick woman and a man with*

leprosy
★ *People plan to kill Jesus*
★ *Jesus dies on a cross*
★ *Jesus comes back to life*

Help the groups that are struggling, by giving them clues. Which do you think was the most significant event in Jesus' life? Ask the groups to give each statement a mark out of ten based upon how significant they feel each one is according to what Jesus accomplished by living. Spend time discussing their answers.

⏸ Pause
(10 mins):
Read John 15:13: 'Greater love has no-one than this, that he lay down his life for his friends.' Talk about how important it was that Jesus died on the cross. In fact, the whole reason he came was to die. Ask the group to explain why he was willing to die for us.

The story of the loving father
A group was once out for a walk along the white cliffs of Dover. At one point the path was narrow and rocky and the fence on one side was in need of repair. A little girl wandered ahead of the party. Turning to see where her father was, she slipped against the fence. The fence gave way and the girl began to slide down a short embankment. At the end of this short embankment was a vertical drop of several hundred feet. She was slipping to certain death. The father, seeing his daughter slipping, without any thought for his own life or the risk involved, jumped over the fence and sprinted to his daughter, catching her on the edge of the precipice. He miraculously saved her and managed not to slip himself even though he had been travelling at speed. The others in the party helped them both to safety.

The father's love drove him to risk his life. Jesus' love drove him to give his life, too, for people who didn't do anything to deserve it. This is the greatest kind of love.

⏩ Fast forward
(5 mins):
Finish by reading Philippians 1:21: 'For me, to live is Christ and to die is gain.' Christ died for our gain. The thousands of people that have died during wars have also died for our gain.

Finish by praying, giving thanks for the people who have laid down their lives for us. Pray that the world would know Christ and therefore true peace.

87

The Christmas promise (1)

outline
34

Aim:

To show how through the coming of Jesus we can not only have a full life but an eternal friendship with God.

You will need: four boxes and items for the *Play* section.

Tuning in
(15 mins):
Pictionary

Split the young people into small groups. Give some paper and pens to each group. Ask a volunteer from each group to collect the first word from the list below. They must then return to their group and draw the object. Once a member of the group has guessed it, they come to the leader for the next word and so on until all the words have been guessed.

Santa; Christmas tree; Shepherd; Christmas cards; Angel; Donkey; Christmas pudding; Holly; Turkey (make up more of your own if you wish).

Party Games

Play some fun party games appropriate to Christmas.

Play
(15 mins):

Start by asking if anyone has an Advent Calendar. Ask them how many days it is to Christmas and if they are looking forward to it.

Advent boxes

Cover four boxes with Christmas paper and put one of the following four items in each:

★ *A selection of Christmas cards*
★ *A video*
★ *Some food*
★ *8 slips of paper with the following written on them:* sweet; happiness; a small gift; eternal life; a true friend; security; satisfaction; Jesus, [written on a scruffy scrap of paper and kept hidden till needed].

Start by asking what comes into people's minds when you say the word 'Christmas'. Show the four boxes and tell them that they are going to have a look in each. Ask for a volunteer to open each box. Go through the first three boxes talking a bit about how these things have become associated with Christmas.

Open the fourth box and read out the list of the first seven presents. How much are they worth? Allocate £10 to each group and hold an auction in which they can bid for each item. How did they choose to spend their money? Discuss which items may give immediate satisfaction and contrast these with those gifts that have lasting value.

Pause

(10 mins):

Go back to the fourth box and 'discover' that there is one more present you hadn't noticed. Apologise, then open it to reveal the word 'Jesus'. Read out John 14:6: 'Jesus answered, "I am the way and the truth and the life. No one comes to the Father except through me."'

Briefly talk about how/why we forget that it is Jesus' birthday we are celebrating. Jesus came to give us life. When we know him as a friend and follow him, we find him in: happiness; satisfaction; a true friend; security; eternal life.

In their groups get them to discuss how Jesus gives us each of these.

Fast forward

(5 mins):
Eternal life

Remind them of the verse 'I am the way and the truth and the life.' Talk about how Jesus came so that we might have the opportunity to have a relationship with God that will last for ever. A good way to do this would be by asking someone to give their testimony, talking about some of the good gifts that Jesus has given them.

The Christmas promise (2)

Aim:

To look at Christmas from the view of those involved at the time.

You will need: wrapping paper; sticky tape, cracker.

Tuning in
(10 mins):
Present wrap

Split the pupils into smaller groups. Give each group some wrapping paper and sticky tape. Ask them to wrap up any item to hand and then pass it round to the other groups. Before opening them each group has to guess what the wrapped items are. As you unwrap the objects explain that today you are going to be unwrapping Christmas to discover what it really is all about.

Play
(30 mins):
On the spot

Give each person in the room a character that is connected to the Christmas story – Joseph, Mary, Shepherds, Innkeeper, Herod, Wise Men, Gabriel, Angels. (If you have a large group it is fine to have two sets of each. Try to make sure that those who know the story well have the larger roles.) Choose one person to be the interviewer in the style of a chat show host. (Ideally, choose a confident person who can improvise and who is familiar with the whole of the Christmas story.) Set the room up as for a chat show and then get your host to introduce their first guest. The rest of the characters make up

the audience until it is their turn to be interviewed.

The show should run smoothly allowing the host to ask each guest a number of open-ended questions such as:

★ *What did you think when...?*
★ *How did you feel when...?*
★ *What happened?*

It is good to allow the audience to ask questions too.

(The aim here is to get into character to try to capture some of the tension and drama of: discovering that your girlfriend is pregnant; being woken by a chorus of angels; being born in a smelly stable, etc.)

It's a cracker

Ask for a couple of volunteers to come and pull a cracker. After they have done that, point out how the ingredients of the cracker can help us to remember what the real message of Christmas is all about:

★ *The Bang*
The surprise that the Shepherds experienced on the hillside.
★ *The Hat*
In the shape of a crown... to remind us that Jesus was a king.

★ *The Toy*
  A present/gift to remind us of the gifts that the
  Wise Men brought.
★ *The Joke*

Sometimes a motto or message... A reminder of
the Christmas message that God loved us so
much that he sent his only son, Jesus, to live
among us.

Fast forward

(5 mins):

The chat show gave us a real insight to
the way in which the original characters reacted to
the birth of the baby Jesus. But what about us?
How do we react to Jesus' birth? Do we ignore it?
Do we celebrate it? Display a selection of Christmas
cards and point out how few of them are in any way
connected to the original Christmas story. Close by
praying that God will help you remember the real
reason for the school holidays and the celebrations
that go on in them. Remind them of how the
cracker can help them do that.
(The Christmas cracker illustration is adapted from
Line Up for Assembly by Jo Pitkin, SU.)

St Valentine's Day

outline
36

Aim:

To look at how God loves us.

Tuning in
(15 mins):

Start off by telling the group that they are going to look at a very popular subject. In fact more songs are written about this subject than any other. See if any one can guess what it might be.

Tell them you are going to think about love. Ask if anyone received a Valentine's card. Do they know whom it's from? Find out how they felt when they got it. It would be worthwhile talking about receiving a Valentine's card yourself and how it made you feel special, loved and accepted. (This works well if you build up the anticipation of the postman coming up the path and exaggerate how you felt on receiving it.) Do remember to be sensitive, however, when asking these questions. Often it's a big deal in school to receive a Valentine's card and those who haven't can feel very *un*special.

The fact is, we all need to be loved. No matter who we are, we all have the basic need to be loved, accepted, noticed, cared for, etc. Ask the group how we show people we love them. Get different suggestions.

When you've heard their suggestions go on to say that we might show love in the following ways:

★ *Flowers*
★ *Chocolates*
★ *Simply showing interest or concern*
★ *Poem (read out a short love poem)*
★ *A kiss*

Tell the group that one romantic way of showing love is by a kiss. Ask for a show of hands if they have ever been kissed. Point out that this includes by parents, grandparents, etc. It may not have been the most enjoyable experience ever but we have all kissed someone. Seeing as we are all experts on kissing therefore, do the following quiz. Clear a space in the middle of the room and tell them that you are going to give two possible answers to each question. They have to guess the correct one. They do this by standing at either side of the room according to the answer you have attributed to that end.

Kiss and make up !!!
1　What is the longest ever screen kiss?
　 (**185 seconds**/255 seconds)
2　What is the longest underwater kiss?
　 (3 min 18 sec/**2 min 18 sec**)
3　A lingering kiss exercises 29 facial muscles.
　 (**True** or false?)
4　What is the record for the longest kiss ever?
　 (15 days/**17 days**)

5   In London 59% of people kiss on the lips each day, where as in Scotland only 38% do. (**True** or false?)

6   Kissing cuts tooth decay. (**True** or false?)

7   Each kiss burns up more than three calories. (True or false?)

8   How many types of bacteria are exchanged when 2 people kiss? (150/**250**)

9   More men keep their eyes closed when kissing than women. (**True** or false!)

Play
(10 mins):
The perfect girlfriend/boyfriend

Split the group into smaller groups, preferably of the same sex. Hand out a large sheet of paper and pens to each group. Ask them to draw a picture of either a boy or girl (the boys draw a girl and the girls draw a boy). Ask them then to write down what the ideal boyfriend/girlfriend would be like and how they would behave/demonstrate their affection. It is worthwhile going round the groups keeping them on track and encouraging deeper comments such as 'someone to talk to', rather than just 'good looking', etc. After a while briefly give each group a chance to feed back to the others.

Pause
(10 mins):

Read 1 John 4:9,10: 'This is how God showed his love among us; He sent his one and only Son into the world that we might live through him. This is love: not that we loved God, but that he loved us ...' Comment on how God loves us simply for who we are and that each one of us is special in his eyes.

In the same groups as before have another look at the boyfriend/girlfriend pictures they have drawn. Ask them to circle with a different-coloured pen those things that they have written which they think are also a way in which God shows he loves us. When they have finished this task, ask them to add any more ways that God shows he loves us. Spend time feeding back from the groups. Conclude by emphasising how God's love is perfect compared to the human mistakes we make in relationships. Boy/girlfriends will let us down in many ways but God never will.

Fast forward
(10 mins):

Remind the group of the ways they decided we might show someone we love them:

★ *Flowers*
★ *Chocolates*
★ *Simply showing interest or concern*
★ *Poem (read out a short love poem)*
★ *A kiss*

Take a vote on which they think is most important.

If that is how *we* show love, how does God show *his* love?

Go back to the verse you read earlier – 'This is how God showed his love among us: He sent his one and only Son into the world that we might live through him.' We show love by flowers, chocolates, etc but God shows his love by sending his own son, Jesus, to die for each one of us. It was something we didn't deserve but God did it anyway. That's how special he thinks you are!

outline 37 Pancakes and ashes

Aim:

To give an understanding of the significance of Shrove Tuesday and Ash Wednesday.

You will need: activity sheet (see p105); frying pan(s), two table tennis balls, pancake ingredients (optional).

Tuning in
(10 mins):
Call my bluff

Photocopy the activity sheet and choose three people to read out the A, B and C possibilities from the *Call my bluff* exercise. After each question, ask one or two of the group which one they think is the correct answer and ask them to give reasons for this. Then take a vote from the whole group.

The correct answers are:

1   B. In the Middle Ages, people went to church to be shriven (forgiven) by their priest before Lent started. Shrove is simply the past tense of the verb 'to shrive'.

2   A. Although Lent actually lasts for forty days, this does not include Sundays so the actual period is longer.

3   C. Yes, people actually burnt wooden crosses and then rubbed the ashes on their face to show that they were sad.

4   A. Pancakes are made of fatty foods and, as people could not eat these during Lent, they needed to eat them up before it started. With no fridges or freezers, the food would have gone off and been wasted otherwise.

5   B. People give things up for Lent as a way of imitating Jesus who went without food for the forty days he spent in the desert (Luke 4:1–2).

Pause
(10 mins):
You decide

Traditionally Christians have used the time of Lent (which starts on Ash Wednesday and goes on until Easter), to live a more simple lifestyle and to spend more time in prayer and Bible study.

Split into smaller groups and discuss the following questions:

★ *Why do you think they do this?*
★ *Why don't they live like this all the year round?*
★ *What changes might you make for the period of Lent?*
★ *What can you do to try to stick to your resolutions?*

Play
(20 mins):
Pancakes!

If you are able, you could arrange with a teacher to go to the Home Economics department and make some pancakes, using the recipe on the next page. Obviously, you will need to get permission for this beforehand and you will also need to arrange getting and bringing in the ingredients. (Although this may be quite an effort, it will definitely be great fun and could be a very effective way of bringing your group together.) If you're not able to do this at school, you might want to have this meeting at someone's house after school and use their kitchen.

If you are not in a position to do this at all, however, you could organise a game in the room whereby you blindfold a person, give them a frying pan and see how many times they can successfully toss and catch a slim book. As a variant, you could see who can toss a pencil case the highest or – if you are really adventurous – you could bring in two pans and organise a relay race with the teams having to toss/bounce a table tennis ball in their pans as they go. You could do this outdoors if there is no room in your regular meeting room.

If you can't go outside and are restricted in the amount of space you have or the amount of noise you are able to make, then you could give everyone a copy of the Activity Sheet and have a go at the activities at the bottom.

Pancake Recipe

125g (4 oz) Plain flour
Pinch of salt
1 egg
1/2 pint of milk
Vegetable oil
Sugar/lemon juice

1   Sift flour into a bowl. Make a well in the centre.

Break in the egg and beat well. Gradually add in the milk as you beat. Mix well.

2   Heat a little of the oil in a frying pan, ensuring there is just enough to cover the base.

3   Add enough batter to coat the base of the pan. Cook for 1–2 mins. Toss and cook until the second side is golden brown.

 Fast forward
(5 mins):
All change?

Remind the group that Pancake Day is a lot of fun but that it is also quite a serious time for Christians as it comes before Ash Wednesday, the beginning of Lent, when they remember the simple lifestyle that Christ led and, to a degree, try to follow in his footsteps. Have a time of silence when the group can think about changes they could make in their busy lives to get closer to God. (Encourage them to think of changes that are realistic, ie giving away all their lunch money for a month may be beyond them, but giving away the 30p that they normally spend on chocolate to a charity might be attainable.) Close with a short prayer, asking God to help them to stick by any decisions that they have made.

Easter

Aim:

To show the significance of the Easter story.

You will need: Easter eggs, *Jesus* or *Jesus of Nazareth* video (optional)

Tuning in
(10 mins):
Who's guilty?

Start the meeting by announcing that the group is in trouble. After last week's meeting, some graffiti was found on a desk and it could only have been done by someone in the group. Explain how disappointed and let down you feel. Will anyone own up? Wait for a few moments. Explain that if no one owns up, it will be necessary to keep everyone in over break and possibly even write to parents. (If this scenario is unrealistic for your situation then simply change it to one that is more likely.)

At this point, one of your group (with whom you have previously arranged this) owns up and admits that they did it. Call them to the front and explain that they will have to go and see the Head of Year (or equivalent) to receive their due punishment. Then say that you find it very difficult to believe that it was them. Did they really do it? Give your accomplice the chance to explain that no, they didn't do it but, in order to save everyone else from the punishment, they are willing to take that punishment on themselves.

Stop the role play at this point and explain to your group – if they haven't already guessed – that the whole thing was a set-up. There was no graffiti

and there will be no punishments. The situation was arranged, however, because it gives a good picture of what Easter is all about. Jesus, who had done no wrong in his life, went to the cross where he took the punishment for all the wrong things that everyone else had done. He volunteered to be punished so that everyone else could go free.

Pause
(20 mins):
Crucified

If you have access to a video, it would be good to show the story of Jesus' crucifixion. There are a number of versions available, eg *Jesus* or *Jesus of Nazareth* – ask at church, your local Christian bookshop or try your school's library or RE department. If you can't get a video, then read the story from Luke 23:32–49 with different people reading the parts of narrator, Jesus, the two thieves and the centurion.

Divide into groups and discuss the following questions:

★ *Why was Jesus crucified?*
★ *Why could this possibly be called a Good Friday?*
★ *What do Christians believe happened to Jesus on Easter Sunday morning?*
★ *Why do Christians believe this is so significant?*

Take some feedback from the groups and then explain that it is a Good Friday because, on it, Jesus was crucified to save people from the punishment they were due for their wrongdoing (sin). So it was good for them and is good for us, even if it wasn't so good for Jesus. He rose again to life on Easter Sunday and so proved that God has authority over death. Through this he opened up the possibility of everlasting life. Christians believe that if they put their trust in Jesus, they will be forgiven for their wrongdoing and one day will live eternally with him in heaven.

Play
(10 mins):
Raised?

In 1 Corinthians 15:17, the apostle Paul says 'If Christ has not been raised, (y)our faith is futile.' Throughout the centuries, people have come up with alternative ideas of what happened to Jesus' body. In the same groups, ask what other explanations they can come up with. Listen to their ideas. The most common explanation is that the disciples took the body, hid it and then started the story of the resurrection. But Jesus actually appeared to many people after this and the disciples were all killed because of their faith in Jesus' resurrection. They would never have been prepared to die for their faith if they knew it to be a lie. The only conclusion Paul could come to is in 1 Corinthians 15:20 where he writes, 'but Christ has indeed been raised ...' You might like to read chapter 4 of *It Makes Sense* (see Appendix for details) for a fuller explanation of the apologetics of the resurrection.

Fast forward
(5 mins):
Prayer time

Invite the group to think seriously about the message of Easter. Have a time of quiet where they can reflect on the fact that Jesus took the punishment for their wrongdoing so that they can be forgiven and be in relationship with God. Close with a prayer where you thank Jesus for his selfless love and for his desire to be friends with us. (Make sure that you are available afterwards to talk with any of the group who want to discuss any of this in more detail. It would also be good if you had some leaflets available that explained the meaning of the cross.)

Finish by giving out a small Easter egg to everyone and wishing them a Happy Easter!

outline

39

Pentecost

Aim:

To look at how the first Pentecost affected the early church.

Tuning in
(10 mins):
Categories

Split everyone into smaller groups. Give each group a pen and paper and call out one of the following categories in turn. The first group to write down the allocated number of suggestions for that category is the winner. Award points accordingly.

Categories:

8 different boys names
7 different sports
14 different colours
5 things we look forward to

(Make up some of your own if you wish but make sure that you finish with the five things we look forward to.)

Say that you're going to look at Pentecost from a before, during and after perspective. Ask the group for suggestions of any more things we look forward to. From the things suggested ask why they would look forward to them. Bring out the excitement and expectancy, etc.

Before

Read John 16:7: 'Unless I go away, the Counsellor will not come to you; but if I go I will send him to you.' Expand on the verse, pointing out how Jesus was soon going to leave them (to die) but that he was sending someone to help them. Parallel the excitement and expectancy we might have for the things mentioned already to that which the disciples would also have felt waiting for the gift that Jesus had promised.

Play
(15 mins):

Give the groups a large sheet of paper and pens. Ask them to imagine that the President of the USA is coming to visit the school. Would he come alone? Who else might accompany him? What might the school do to welcome him? What would happen as he arrived?

During

Ask the group how they think the person Jesus was talking about would have come. Can they picture it?

Read Acts 2:1–14. (*The Dramatised Bible* version works well for this.)

Explain that this is called Pentecost. Expand on how the Holy Spirit came so dramatically and that this was the point at which the Christian church really started growing.

Pause

(15 mins):
After

The Holy Spirit played a key role in forming the church. Say to the group that we are going to look at the difference the Holy Spirit made. Photocopy the following statements. Ask the group to work in pairs (with one set of statements between them). Have the missing words from each statement spread around the room. Tell the group they have to work out which word fits into which statement.

1   Helped the church to _ _ _ _ bigger **(grow)**
2   _ _ _ _ _ _ the church when things were difficult **(helped)**
3   _ _ _ _ _ _ _ _ more about God to the church **(revealed)**
4   Showed the _ _ _ _ _ _ _ way to live **(correct)**
5   Gave the church _ _ _ _ _ to do things **(power)**
6   _ _ _ _ _ _ the church in the right direction **(guided)**

(Think up some more of your own if you wish.)
Allow time to feed back on what the statements say about the Holy Spirit. He still does these things in the church today.

Fast forward

(5 mins):
What is that?

Finish by playing *What is that?* Divide into small groups and give each one the name of an object that you would find in a church, eg pulpit, chair. The group then has to make the shape of that article using their bodies while the rest of the groups have to try to guess what the article is. Emphasise that the different articles are made out of people. The church is not a physical building but a body of people. Therefore, when the Holy Spirit helps the church, he does so by working in the lives of individual Christians, building them into a body together.

Exams

Aim:

To show how God is interested in every part of our lives and that he has a plan for each one of us.

Tuning in
(10 mins):
Inventors game

Tell the group that they are going to be thinking about exams – something we would all like to avoid. Go on to ask if anyone in the group has thought about becoming a scientist. Scientists have made great discoveries and inventions. (Write the following inventions and discoveries on a board/OHP with the solutions mixed up.) In groups, they are to match the following inventions/discoveries to the right inventor.

Telephone	G Alexander Bell
TV	John Logie Baird
Penicillin	Fleming
Electromagnetism	Maxwell
Ultrasound	Ian Donald
Steam engine	James Watt
Raincoats	Mackintosh
Antiseptics	Lister
Transatlantic telephone link	Kelvin

Hard work

Talk about how each invention came as the result of much hard work over time and, sadly, the same is true for exam success. In order for us to do well in exams we need to put in some effort. We cannot sit back and expect success to come to us. We need to do a healthy amount of work!

Play
(20 mins):
Under pressure

Ask the group if they feel, or have felt under pressure to do well in exams. Where does the pressure come from? Read out the following four main areas of pressure then take a vote on which the group feel is the greatest source of pressure:

★ *Friends*
★ *Family*
★ *Media*
★ *School*

Bring out how they may feel pressurised by each of these different areas at different times and sometimes by several at the same time. Although sometimes it is not a healthy pressure, not all pressure needs to be negative. Some pressure is good. We often achieve more when under a bit of pressure, eg a deadline. It's *excessive* pressure that is unhealthy.

Group work

In small groups answer the following:
1 What would your dream be for the future if you could do anything?
2 Who would you go to for help about exam pressure?

3 How would you expect an ideal friend to help you cope with exams?

Pause
(10 mins):

After getting feedback from the groups, read Psalm 121. Ask the groups if anyone considered God as someone who could help them. Discuss the list of things they have written about how a good friend can help them and link those to the character and actions of God.

Unsuspecting volunteer

Sitting in a circle, give each person a piece of paper. At the top ask them to put the name of another person in the group. On a given signal, everyone folds over their paper and passes it on clockwise. Underneath the name (which is now hidden), the next person should put the name of a school subject (eg maths). Again, the papers are folded over and passed on. This time the group writes either *Expects to pass* or *Expects to fail* before folding over and passing on again. The fourth time, the group writes either *Passed* or *Failed* and folds and passes again. Then the group opens their papers and reads them out to discover their consequences.

Explain that some people will expect to pass their exams – and will. Others may expect to fail – and will. But there are some who will face either unexpected joy or unexpected disappointment. It is important to remember that God will always be

with you to share in the joys and to help you through the disappointments. His love and care for you doesn't waver whether you achieve lots or you fail.

Fast forward
(5 mins):
Discuss

Talk about how God knows all about the future and nothing surprises him. In an unsure world, where we don't know how things will turn out, we can always go to God. We can ask him for guidance and help to deal with unexpected things in life.

Activity Sheet
The environment

A. In your house do you:

★ Recycle your newspapers?
★ Recycle your glass?
★ Take litter away with you?
★ Save your aluminium cans?
★ Put your compost in your garden?

List three other things that you do to care for the environment:

★
★
★

B. Cross out all the W, X, and Zs in the following sentence to discover what the Bible has to say about the earth.

XTHWE ZEZARWXTHW IZS WTWHEZ
XLOXRZWDSW AWXNZD
EVXWERWYWTHZXIXNGW WXIZN IZT.
(ZPWSWALXM 2Z4:W1)

C. Write a prayer in the leaf that reflects your concern for the environment.

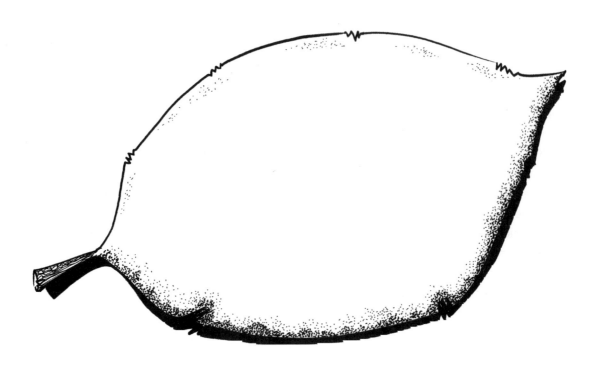

Activity Sheet
Self worth

A. Score the following ideas on a scale of 1–5, where:

1 = No value 2 = Little value 3 = Some value
4 = Considerable value 5 = Great value.

The world places X value on people according to:

What car they drive	___
Their honesty	___
Where they go on holiday	___
Their house	___
Their friends	___
Their qualifications	___
Their friendliness	___
Their clothes	___
Their experience	___
Their income	___
A strong marriage	___
Their career	___
Their faith in God	___

B. Decide what these Bible verses say about the value that God places on us.

'So God created man in his own image, in the image of God he created him; male and female he created them.' (Genesis 1:27)

'For you created my inmost being; you knit me together in my mother's womb. I praise you because I am fearfully and wonderfully made; your works are wonderful, I know that full well. My frame was not hidden from you when I was made in the secret place. When I was woven together in the depths of the earth, your eyes saw my unformed body. All the days ordained for me were written in your book before one of them came to be.' (Psalm 139:13–16)

'Look at the birds of the air; they do not sow or reap or store away in barns, and yet your heavenly Father feeds them. Are you not much more valuable than they?' (Matthew 6:26)

'Are not two sparrows sold for a penny? Yet not one of them will fall to the ground apart from the will of your Father. And even the very hairs of your head are all numbered. So don't be afraid; you are worth more than many sparrows.' (Matthew 10:29–31)

'This is how we know what love is: Jesus Christ laid down his life for us …' (1 John 3:16)

C. Discuss the following three questions:

1 What things does the world value most?

2 From the Bible passages above, explain why we are valuable to God.

3 Decide whether our true value lies in what we do or in who we are.

Activity Sheet
Harvest

Favourite foods

1   Someone who likes beans

2   Someone who likes apples

3   Someone who likes prunes

4   Someone who likes pineapple

5   Someone who likes coconut

6   Someone who likes bananas

7   Someone who likes oranges

8   Someone who likes blackberries

9   Someone who likes gooseberries

10 Someone who likes pears

Activity Sheet
Pancakes and ashes

Call my bluff

1 Shrove Tuesday is called Shrove because:

a) in olden times, pancakes were actually called shroves.

b) in olden times people went to church on this day to be shriven, meaning forgiven.

c) shrove is actually a misspelling of the Hebrew word 'Shroade', meaning 'pancake'.

2 The period which is known as Lent actually lasts:

a) less than forty days.

b) forty days exactly.

c) more than 40 days.

3 Ash Wednesday is called Ash Wednesday because:

a) in olden times people rubbed ashes on their faces.

b) traditionally, people gave up smoking and so it was called No Ash Wednesday.

c) on this day people wore sackcloth – a new fashion. Fashion Wednesday became Ash Wednesday.

4 People eat pancakes on Shrove Tuesday because:

a) they wanted to eat up all their high calorie foods before Lent started.

b) cleaning frying pans was a way for children to earn money in Lent. So the parents made sure that they got them really dirty before it started.

c) each village used to hold a competition to see who could eat the most pancakes on this day.

5 People give up things for Lent because:

a) it was a time when they gave things away or lent them to friends.

b) Jesus gave up food for forty days when he was in the desert.

c) they know they're going to eat loads of chocolate over Easter so they go on a diet beforehand.

Just for fun

How many words can you make from the word 'Pancake'? (They must have three letters or more.) Changing just one letter at a time and ensuring that you always have proper words, can you get from L O V E to L I FE? (Easy.) How about from D E A D to L I F E? (Not so easy.)

Crack the wordsearch (backwards, forwards and diagonally) to discover the following words that all have an Easter connection: nails; thieves; cross; Sunday; Jesus; forgiven; risen; love; sin; hope.

R	I	S	V	N	A	L	P	I
I	H	Y	A	D	N	U	S	J
L	R	I	E	S	N	O	F	E
E	L	T	H	I	E	V	E	S
S	T	M	L	S	V	P	V	U
G	N	N	L	C	I	F	O	S
P	K	E	W	R	G	U	L	H
O	A	S	S	O	R	C	T	U
B	I	I	V	L	O	A	R	T
N	R	R	B	Z	F	H	B	O

Illustrations for **'What is sin?'** outline.

Apple

People

Illustrations for **'What is sin?'** outline, continued.

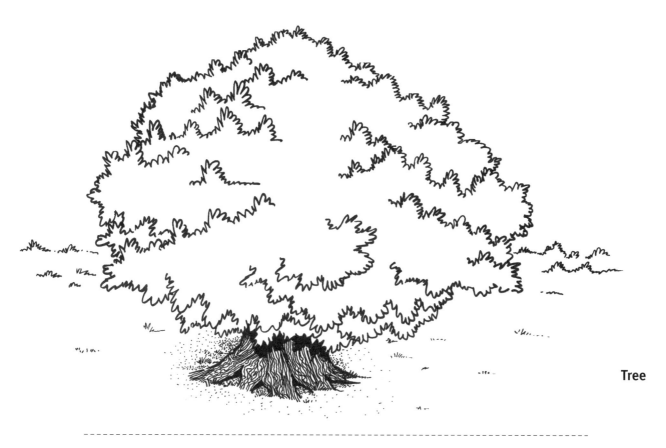

Tree

Going to church

Illustrations for **'Fellowship and growth'** outline.

107

Illustrations for **'Fellowship and growth'** outline, continued.

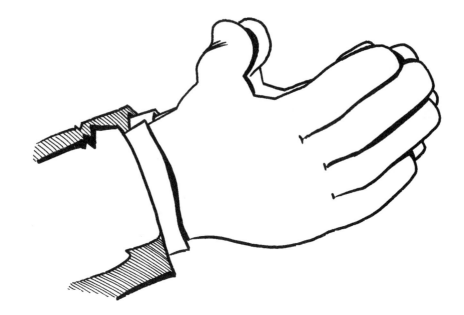

Praying to God

Reading the Bible

Illustrations for **'Following Jesus'** outline.

Illustrations for **'Guidance'** outline.

Appendix of further resources

To order any of these resources, please contact Scripture Union Mail Order, PO Box 764, Oxford, OX4 5FJ (Tel: 01865 716880, Fax: 01865 715152, email: su.mailbox@lion-publishing.co.uk).

For more information or a catalogue please contact the Sales and Promotions Department, Scripture Union, 207–209 Queensway, Bletchley, Milton Keynes, MK2 2EB (Tel: 01908 856182, email: info@scriptureunion.org,uk).

Books:

The Schools Work Handbook by Emlyn Williams (£5.99): A practical guide for anyone who wants to serve God in schools, which will also be helpful to those already involved to develop their ministry.

...Just Think About That! by Phil Wason (£7.99): Forty tried and tested, ready-to-use assembly outlines to help you challenge, captivate and encourage young people at secondary school.

Everyone Can Know by Andrew Smith, Jeannie Poulton and John Hayward (£10.00, A4): 30 ready-to-use assembly outlines for use in multi-faith schools. Mainly for use with pupils in Key Stage 2 (8s to 11s) although some can be used with Key Stage 3 (11s to 14s).

Pitstop by Steve Bullock (£7.99, A4): A resource book with 20 complete session outlines for 11s to 13s as well as advice on running a Christian club, faith development, safety in the group, etc.

Shock Tactics by Peter Graystone, Paul Sharp and Pippa Turner (£5.99, A4): Bible study resources for groups of over 13s, designed to encourage creative discussion and prayer.

YoYo 2 and YoYo 4 by Peter Graystone, Paul Sharp and Pippa Turner (£3.95, A4): A fantastic resource programme packed with ideas for over-13s. It has a unique choice of three approaches to each topic – you choose the one that meets the needs of your individual group. Eight programmes in each book including discussion starters, imaginative approaches to worship and worksheets.

Rap, Rhyme & Reason by Anita Haigh (£4.99): A collection of monologues, poems, sketches and raps based on Jesus' teaching. This resource can be used in schools, youth groups and family services to encourage young people to reflect on key issues like justice, forgiveness, fear, anger and faith, and to think about what Jesus said for themselves.

'Get A Life' and other sketches for your youth group by Tony Bower, Edmund Farrow and Matt Sands (£6.99, A4): A collection of 15 new sketches for youth groups to perform during group meetings or larger youth events. All the sketches are Bible-based and explore issues that are relevant to young people today.

Sound Foundation: Living God's way in God's world by Dennis Pethers (£12.99 per pack). A youth-friendly introduction to Christianity in the format of a five-week course. Cells are run by a group member, with a youth leader overseeing one or more cells. Packs contain five magazines for those attending the course, one cell leader's guide and one youth leader's guide.

Mind Games by Simon Hall (£5.99). This easy-to-use, exciting collection of resources is designed to stimulate learning in ways that are more creative and imaginative, helping youth to learn about and worship God, and to get into the Bible. Over 50 tried and tested, ready-to-use activities.

The Expanded Chocolate Teapot by David Lawrence (£3.50): The classic guide to surviving as a Christian at school, now with two new chapters: how (not) to start your new career at secondary school, and what to do when you feel you have let God down.

The Superglue Sandwich by David Lawrence (£3.99): If friends at school ask you 'Did God really make the world?' or 'Is the Bible really true?', what do you say? David Lawrence offers clues to the answers to these and other similar questions.

It Makes Sense by Stephen Gaukroger (£3.50): This newly updated edition of Stephen Gaukroger's best-selling book offers a humorous and compelling look at the reasons why it does make sense to be a Christian. Covers science, suffering, other faiths and a host of other issues.

Videos

The Challenger The Champion (£14.99): Words, music and pictures combine to present the life of Jesus in a powerful and moving way.

How to Beat the System (£14.99): Two light-hearted productions for 11s to 15s which help to break down preconceived ideas about the Bible and prayer.

Joseph (£14.99): In the course of four episodes, we see how God's plan works out in the life of Joseph, from the time when he first starts talking about his dream to the day when, as Governor of Egypt, he is reunited with this father.

Speak for Yourself (£14.99): A 3-part documentary-style video. In short fast-paced sound bites six older teens/early twenties Christians explain what God means to them, how they came to faith, and the difference being a Christian has made to their lives. An excellent discussion starter.

Bible reading resources

Dated material:

One Up for 11 to 14 year olds (£2.30 per quarter). Daily Bible readings in an up-to-date teen magazine format in full colour, with a problem page, cartoons and music reviews.

Revving Up is the free sample of **One Up** Bible reading notes.

disclosure: go one on one with God (£2.50 per issue) for the 15+ age group. Published bi-monthly, **disclosure** is a radically different Bible reading guide in contemporary style and format with readings for every weekday, and special articles on relevant issues, group discussion starters, music, film and TV reviews. Free sample available from Scripture Union Sales and Promotions Department.

Leaflets/Booklets

Big Questions by David Lawrence (£0.60 each. Outreach packs available: 20 pack - £12.00, 60 pack – £30.00, 100 pack – £45.00.)

The following free leaflets are available from Scripture Union's Schools Department:

Is your church ready for school?

Praying for schools.

Starting and leading Christian groups in schools.

For more information please contact Clare Hornett, Scripture Union Schools Department, 207–209 Queensway, Bletchley, Milton Keynes, MK2 2EB.

Other agencies that produce useful material include:

Covenanters, 11 Lower Hillgate, Stockport, SK1 1JQ Tel: 0161 474 1262

Crusaders, 2 Romeland Hill, St Albans, AL3 4ET Tel: 01727 855 422

CTVC, Hillside Studios, Merry Hill Road, Bushey, Watford, WD2 1DR Tel: 0181 950 4426

CPAS, Athena Drive, Tachbrook Park, Warwick, CV34 6NG Tel: 01926 458 458

Discovery (part of Agapé), Fairgate House, Kings Road, Tyseley, Birmingham, B11 2AA Tel: 0121 441 3364

Oasis Trust, 87 Blackfriars Road, London, SE1 8HA Tel: 0171 928 9422

Oxfam, 274 Banbury Road, Oxford, OX2 7DZ Tel: 01865 311 311

Tear Fund, 100 Church Road, Teddington TW11 8QE Tel: 0181 977 9144

World Vision UK, 599 Avebury Boulevard, Milton Keynes, MK9 3PG Tel: 01908 841 000

Youth For Christ, PO Box 5254, Halesowen, B63 3DG Tel: 0121 550 8055

Youthwork Magazine, 37 Elm Road, New Malden, KT3 3HB Tel: 0181 942 9761

Youth With A Mission, Highfield Oval, Ambrose Lane, Harpenden, AL5 4BX

It is also well worth checking out your local Christian bookshop for other ideas and resources.